Praise for *Raising Resilience*

"In *Raising Resilience* Chris Willard beautifully bridges between East and West, ancient philosophy and modern science. He offers the kind of wisdom families need in these challenging times."

TAL BEN-SHAHAR
author of *Happier: Learn the Secrets to Daily Joy and Lasting Fulfillment*

"A beautiful combination of ancient wisdom, current neuroscience, and authentic parenting stories, *Raising Resilience* is a helpful guide full of practices to cultivate goodness and healthy development in our children."

TINA PAYNE BRYSON, PHD
coauthor of *The Whole-Brain Child* and *No-Drama Discipline*

"I love this book. We know that children do better when they feel better, and so do adults. How often do we expect children to control their behaviors when we haven't learned to control our own—even though we know that example is the best teacher? In this book you will learn strategies for developing beautiful values/principles in your own life, as well as how to teach them to your children. Guaranteed to help you and your children feel better and do better."

DR. JANE NELSEN
coauthor of the *Positive Discipline* series

"A tour de force! Seamlessly written, the author integrates timeless wisdom and modern science into the heart of family life. This book is an indispensable companion for parents who want to cultivate goodness in themselves and their children."

CHRISTOPHER GERMER, PHD
author of *The Mindful Path to Self-Compassion*

"In *Raising Resilience*, parents around the world will find tremendous support for meeting the challenges of childrearing. Connecting an ancient list of helpful qualities with the current research demonstrating their usefulness makes a compelling case for putting these ideas into practice."

SHARON SALZBERG
author of *Lovingkindness* and *Real Happiness*

"This book is a great map for wise parenting, written by a clinician willing to weave in his own compelling personal as well as professional experience. It is unique—combining Dr. Willard's years of knowledge and practice with commonsense wisdom and good new tips—all backed by current research studies in psychology and neuroscience."

TRUDY GOODMAN, PHD
founding teacher of InsightLA

"Dr. Willard has offered us another gem that brings together the best of ancient wisdom and modern science on positive youth development and resilience, to help our young people develop into thriving and compassionate adults. As a pediatrician and a mindfulness practitioner and teacher, I will be highly recommending this book to the parents in my work and in my life."

DZUNG X. VO, MD, FAAP
author of *The Mindful Teen: Powerful Skills to Help You Handle Stress One Moment at a Time*

"For any parent seeking wisdom, guidance, and sanity in the midst of raising children, Dr. Willard's *Raising Resilience* provides a unique, practical resource written in a light and enjoyable style."

MARK BERTIN, MD
author of *Mindful Parenting for ADHD: A Guide to Cultivating Calm, Reducing Stress, and Helping Children Thrive*

"This book is a conversation with true friends—the ten perfections of the heart, or guiding principles for parenting. These are the type of friends who bring out the best in us, and are also compassionate and encouraging with us when we fall short of our aspirations. Dr. Willard introduces us to these friends with honesty, humor, and humility. So grab a cup of tea or coffee, and sit down with these friends to laugh, cry, and reflect; you, and your children, will be glad you did."

AMY SALTZMAN, MD
author of *A Still Quiet Place: A Mindfulness Program for Teaching Children and Adolescents to Ease Stress and Difficult Emotions*

"In his wonderful new book, Chris Willard offers parents a set of fun, practical, and wise tools to nurture virtue and values in their children and themselves."

SUSAN KAISER GREENLAND
author of *Mindful Games* and *The Mindful Child*

"A valuable contribution to parent guidance. It will appeal to new parents who are struggling with the demands of nurturing and fostering generosity of spirit."

NANCY RAPPAPORT, MD
associate professor of psychiatry at Harvard Medical School

"In *Raising Resilience* Christopher Willard guides us to master mindfulness in our everyday worlds of tantrums, helicopter parenting, and all the joys and struggles of our modern lives. Instead of seeing family as a disruption to deepening our mindfulness practice, Willard shows us a potent opportunity of cultivating patience, generosity, and wisdom amidst the swirl. With his expertise in mindfulness and psychology, Willard offers a profound exploration of how to cultivate a mindful family amidst the chaos of our modern world, planting compassionate and wise seeds for our children and our future."

DANIEL RECHTSCHAFFEN, MFT
author of *The Way of Mindful Education* and *The Mindful Education Workbook*

"At last, a realistic, pragmatic approach that brings spiritual wisdom to bear on our development as parents. Willard's broad and deep reflections integrate the best of timeless teachings, spot-on personal stories, and up-to-date research. This is a fabulous book!"

SUMI LOUNDON KIM
author of *Sitting Together: A Family-Centered Curriculum on Mindfulness, Meditation, and Buddhist Teachings*

"What a wonderful book! This excellent resource presents the critical relevance of virtues like generosity, ethics, and patience to modern family life and parenting—all supported by comprehensive research and brain science. Dr. Willard has translated age-old wisdom into a trove of reflections, activities, and practical advice to support parents and children in leading happier, more connected lives."

JESSICA MOREY
executive director, Inward Bound Mindfulness Education

"*Raising Resilience* offers remarkably comprehensive, trustworthy, and relevant guidance for living and modeling resilience to today's caring but over-busy parents. Dr. Willard's engaging style, with illuminating examples from his own experience as a clinician and as a parent, make this book a breeze to read, and a reliable companion on the journey toward loving, happy families."

LINDA GRAHAM, MFT
author of *Bouncing Back*

raising
resilience

Also by Christopher Willard, PsyD

Books

Growing Up Mindful: Essential Practices to Help Children, Teens, and Families Find Balance, Calm, and Resilience

Child's Mind: Mindfulness Practices to Help Our Children Be More Focused, Calm, and Relaxed

Mindfulness for Teen Anxiety: A Workbook for Overcoming Anxiety at Home, at School, and Everywhere Else (An Instant Help Book for Teens)

Mindfulness for Teen Depression: A Workbook for Improving Your Mood
coauthored with Mitch Abblett, PhD

Teaching Mindfulness Skills to Kids and Teens
coedited with Amy Saltzman, MD

Audio

Practices for Growing Up Mindful: Guided Meditations and Simple Exercises for Children, Teens, and Families

Cards

The Self-Compassion Deck: 50 Mindfulness-Based Practices,
coauthored with Mitch Abblett, PhD

The Growing Mindful Deck,
coauthored with Mitch Abblett, PhD

The Growing Happy Deck,
coauthored with Mitch Abblett, PhD

The Mindful Reminders Deck,
coauthored with Mitch Abblett, PhD

raising
resilience

THE WISDOM AND SCIENCE OF HAPPY
FAMILIES AND THRIVING CHILDREN

CHRISTOPHER
WILLARD, PSYD

sounds true
BOULDER, COLORADO

Sounds True
Boulder, CO 80306

This book is not intended as a substitute for the medical recommendations of
physicians, mental health professionals, or other health-care providers. Rather, it is
intended to offer information to help the reader cooperate with physicians, mental
health professionals, and health-care providers in a mutual quest for optimal well-
being. We advise readers to carefully review and understand the ideas presented and
to seek the advice of a qualified professional before attempting to use them.

Some names and identifying details have been changed to protect the privacy of
individuals.

Published 2017

Cover design by Rachael Murray
Book design by Beth Skelley

Cover image © Lesyaskripak; shutterstock.com

Printed in Canada

Library of Congress Cataloging-in-Publication Data

Names: Willard, Christopher (Psychologist), author.
Title: Raising resilience : the wisdom and science of happy families and
   thriving children / Christopher Willard, PsyD.
Description: Boulder, CO : Sounds True, [2017] | Includes bibliographical
   references and index.
Identifiers: LCCN 2017002654 (print) | LCCN 2017028521 (ebook) | ISBN
   9781622038688 (ebook) | ISBN 9781622038671 (pbk. : alk. paper)
Subjects: LCSH: Resilience (Personality trait) in children. | Parenting.
Classification: LCC BF723.R46 (ebook) | LCC BF723.R46 W55 2017 (print) | DDC
   170/.44--dc23
LC record available at https://lccn.loc.gov/2017002654

10 9 8 7 6 5 4 3 2 1

For my parents, **Ann and Norman Willard**—
not that you needed a book to raise
resilient kids and grandkids, but I'm sure
I gave you reasons to want one.

contents

off the cushion

Years ago, when my wife was pregnant with our first child, I went to the local meditation center to make an appointment with my teacher, Madeline Klyne. "How on earth am I going to maintain my meditation practice, let alone be a good parent?" I asked over a cup of lukewarm green tea.

Maddy paused and then laughed. "Don't even bother!" she declared with a dismissive wave of her hand. "Let your meditation cushion collect dust for a while, and just focus on what you can do *off* the cushion. Focus on the *paramis*—the ten perfections of the heart."

The paramis—generosity, ethics, renunciation, wisdom, energy, patience, honesty, determination, kindness, and equanimity—are concepts from a number of Eastern philosophies that I believe anyone can get behind, regardless of spiritual (or nonspiritual) background. These days, words like *virtue* and *values* can garner an eye roll given the hypocrisy of so many self-appointed virtuous folks. But perhaps we've thrown the proverbial baby out with the bathwater. I mean, who can really say that they're against such values as honesty and patience? Different cultures may have their own ways of teaching virtues such as these, but what intrigues me is how neuroscience soundly backs not only the benefit of such concepts in achieving lifelong happiness and resilience but also the ability of such concepts to spread virally from person to person.

After the birth of my son, life was undeniably happening *off* my cushion, and my spiritual life had to change—but I believe it was for the better. I dove into this new form of practice, deliberately acting with kindness toward strangers, practicing patience with my family, and simplifying my life by speaking more plainly and honestly about my needs. I was following and living the paramis inside and outside of my family life—or at least I was trying to. I also dove headlong into books and lectures about Eastern philosophy (in addition to the parenting books I was frantically reading). Gradually, I began to piece together a new way of approaching parenthood, spirituality, and the drastically altered landscape of my life as a parent.

These ten virtues might seem straightforward, but they're not always so easy to follow in today's world—neither for ourselves nor for our children. To make matters more difficult, the paramis are often translated as "perfections"—a challenging word for those of us, like me, who compulsively consume parenting books and blogs to make sure we get it all "right." Thus, it may be more helpful to think about these virtues as qualities that we (and our children) are forever perfecting, just like meditation, yoga practice, or even our golf game. We are looking for practice and progress, not perfection. To paraphrase psychologist Elisha Goldstein, we can turn these values into verbs and live them.[1]

What's more, practicing the paramis triggers tremendous benefits in our brains and promotes behaviors that improve the quality of life for us and those around us. Yet each of the ten virtues actually comes hardwired into us. We can understand this fact in various ways: We could use the spiritual metaphor of seeds (karma) that need watering by parents and caregivers. Or we could see it through the lens of evolutionary biology, which asserts that these traits are inscribed in our DNA for survival and that, when we practice the virtues, our genes express themselves in different ways in a process known as epigenetics. Or we could examine the neuroscience and learn that toddlers have three times the neural connections as adults—connections that are "pruned" as children grow. We adults can influence which networks are pruned and which are cultivated, so they use it and don't lose it, with these kinds of values and behaviors. Lastly, we can look at the exciting research in emotional and behavioral contagions—that is, how behaviors and emotions spread from person to person through our mirror neurons and other parts of the brain that we are just now discovering.

As you'll discover in this book, robust research supports the cultivation of these ten values in yourself and your family. For example, generosity rewires the brain to release antidepressant neurotransmitters, and generosity is literally contagious—it positively affects people three degrees of separation away from the giver. Practicing ethical behavior helps children build strong attachments and promotes emotional and physical safety, as well as happiness. Renunciation (meaning fewer activities and less stuff) teaches kids how to compromise, concentrate, and creatively solve problems as those problems arise. Ancient practices for cultivating wisdom mirror what modern scientists recommend for healthy brain development, integrating all parts of the growing brain in order to be flexible and agile. When we encourage our kids' independence and when we teach them to focus their energy on effort over outcome, they grow up to be resilient in the face of life's inevitable challenges.

Of course, we could all use more patience. Learning to delay gratification has been linked to improved executive function, happier relationships, and higher educational and vocational achievement into adulthood. Likewise, practicing honesty leads to more happiness and optimism—not to mention it keeps us out of trouble! The benefits of determination and grit are particularly well known these days, and we can use the power of mindset to cultivate them. Kindness actually changes the shape and structure of the brain, boasting evidence of improved health, happiness, and thriving. Lastly, equanimity—the ability to take life's inevitable challenges in stride—may itself be the very essence of thriving and resilience.

In this book, you'll find a lot of idealized scenarios, as well as some parenting flops of my own. (In case you haven't noticed yet, parenthood doesn't usually work out according to plan.) What this book does not offer, however, is a magic three-step technique or formula, though it does share the causes and conditions that science and spirituality tell us lead to happy, thriving families. I once heard someone say that raising a child is more like tending a garden than creating a flower. As this book illustrates, all we can do is create the conditions under which our children are likely to blossom; we can't force them to bloom in the exact way or time we wish.

Although we tell our kids to do as we say, not as we do, we all watch as our kids imitate us—whether it's the positive, when they say thank you, or the negative, when we realize we need to cut out some of our more colorful language and less-than-healthy behaviors. Research also illustrates, time and again, that behavior is far more contagious than mere words. Thus, *you* are your child's most important model for behavior. The bad news (or the good news, depending on your viewpoint) is that the best way to teach these virtues to your children is by practicing them yourself. You can talk all you want about generosity with your kids, but if you don't model giving and encourage that behavior in your family, it's unlikely to take root.

In fact, the more you live these values in your life, the easier they become. If you're kind today, it becomes easier to be kind tomorrow; if you're unkind today, you are more likely to be unkind tomorrow. As with any physical training, we can build our mental and emotional muscles with practice, but building anything must start with a solid foundation. In addition, it's easier to promote these values in ourselves and our children when our bodies and brains are healthy with the sleep, nutrition, and feelings of safety they need. Remember this when things are going south: if you're hungry, angry, anxious, lonely, or tired, your ability to be at your best will diminish. As Lao-Tzu said, "Put things in order before they appear." In other words, the wisest use of our energy is to cultivate these qualities from the beginning—not just when something goes wrong. So take care of yourself—it will make all the difference down the road.

Is this a spiritual book? Yes and no. If you are a spiritual person, this book will speak to you; but even if you're an avowed scientific atheist, you'll find research aplenty. I understand that any book on values and virtues can easily come off as self-righteous (you likely have enough judgmental friends, relatives, coworkers, and strangers telling you how to parent). My intention here isn't to add to your to-do list. In fact, you may want to consider all the creative ways you are already helping your kids live these values through your family traditions. This isn't intended to be a book telling you what you *should* do; rather, it's a book of ideas for what you *could* do as a parent. My hope is to offer a few more ideas. I examine both Eastern and Western wisdom traditions, weigh them with modern science, and share the surprisingly large overlap of the best practices for raising thriving kids. Here, you'll read stories of the Buddha's helicopter parents, alongside references to Judaism, Christianity, and some of the world's other sources of wisdom.

As I mentioned earlier, although the paramis may be referred to as "perfections," please go easy. In fact, when you push yourself to be too perfect, that effort often backfires in an effect known as "moral licensing," which we look at more in the ethics and honesty chapters (chapters 2 and 7). So set a course for a middle way between not trying enough and trying too hard, knowing that you'll be blown off course from time to time. These are not commandments to make or break; they are aspirations, representing our best selves at our best moments, and we can create the conditions to live up to them. The paramis are about celebrating and bringing out your best; they are not about beating yourself up emotionally for falling short. Likewise, not every suggestion in this book (and these *are* meant to be suggestions) needs to be clung to blindly. If it works for you and your family, great! If not, let it go. Science and the wisdom traditions tell us to experiment and see for ourselves, and I encourage you to do just that.

I hope it's apparent that the values explored in this book aren't just for kids; they're also meant to help us become better parents, a job that often pushes us to become better people—or, perhaps more accurately, imperfect people who are just more effective. Someone recently pointed out to me that we put more effort into parenting than ever before, so here's some advice: Don't just *try* to parent; *be* a parent. Better yet, enjoy the lifelong process of *becoming* a parent. It reminds me of the spiritual axioms that say it's better to be Christ-like than to call yourself a Christian and better to be more Buddha-like than Buddhist—and while we're at it, remember that it's better to act like a saint than to act sanctimoniously.

If you're not familiar with my work, you might be wondering who I am to write a book like this? Well, for starters, just like you, I've been a kid, and I didn't feel like I was very good at it. As I got older, I was a difficult teen who had some challenges and rebellions (some of which you'll hear about). By the time things improved in my mid-twenties, I'd largely returned to the values that my parents had instilled—the seeds had blossomed. My parents (as well as several other important adults in my life) helped plant those seeds in me as a younger child, and they continued to water them during my difficult times until I learned to water them myself. I grew up to become a special education teacher; then psychologist, researcher, writer, professor; and now father who teaches around the world. I've brought all of these experiences into my writing and teaching; in this book, you'll find anecdotes from my own personal and professional life alongside references to the latest science of child development.

Lastly, I want to emphasize that this book is not a formula for greatness. It does not guarantee your child Ivy League admission, a seat on the Supreme Court, or spiritual enlightenment. What it is, is a guide to goodness. Specifically, this book examines how goodness can thrive and even spread through generosity, ethics, renunciation, wisdom, energy, patience, honesty, determination, kindness, and equanimity.

reflection In what ways are you already teaching and practicing these values in your family? What from the list of paramis jumps out at you as challenging for you or your family? What feels natural given your upbringing and values? How can you cultivate goodness in your growing children?

CHAPTER 1

getting through giving

(Raising Generosity—Dāna)

Imagine a two-year-old walking up to you. She has something in her hands that she wants to share with you—perhaps a toy or another treasure. We all know the look on her face and the utter delight of freely offering something—her glowing desire to share her joy. What response does this picture provoke as you imagine it in mind and body? Maybe you find yourself smiling as you bring the image to mind. Now think of this same two-year-old, but this time she wants something from you. I mean, she *really* wants something—say, that stuffed tiger from the advertisement or that chocolate bar from the checkout aisle—but she can't have it. Visualize her response—stomping rage, screaming, inconsolable tears. What's your response now?

Even from a young age, humans are simple. When we act with generosity, we and those around us are happy; when we act with craving and selfishness, we all end up miserable. Yet even when we all know this to be true, it can be so hard to put generosity into practice.

Our children might always struggle with sharing. For that matter, *we* might always struggle with sharing. It doesn't matter—we're all capable of more when we water the seeds of generosity with which we are born. We can actually cultivate the innate generosity in children's brains (and in our brains) by encouraging the neurons of generosity to grow, while pruning the neurons of greed, just as in a garden. Like all natural things, those seeds of generosity (which are there from birth) need attention to grow and blossom. In fact, the instinct to share with parents is one of the first markers of social development.

We're wired to be generous. What's more, science (as well as the cliché) suggests we feel more joy in giving than in receiving.[1]

Greed and yearning are clearly painful, and most spiritual traditions advise against the dangers of craving and coveting. In fact, neuroscience now tells us that wanting and jealousy light up the same receptors in our brains that are stimulated when we experience physical pain.[2] This makes intuitive sense, but think back to the two-year-old. How does it feel to be that child who absolutely *needs* the chocolate bar *right now*?

If generosity feels so good, why do we need help to encourage it? Our genetic blueprint has been evolving for millions of years—nature tells us to want and hoard more than we need in order to survive. What's more, our culture bombards our families with messages that *getting that thing* will make us happy. Even our politicians prescribe retail therapy for emotional pain. George W. Bush famously encouraged Americans to go to Disney World and go shopping after the tragedies of 9/11.[3] All of these messages run counter to the spiritual wisdom and scientific findings that show that health and happiness come more through *giving* than through *getting*.

Our culture and our economic system encourage unlimited desires in a world of limited resources, when what we need is something entirely different—to reduce our consumption in order to live in harmony and compassion with others and the planet. No wonder philosophers and spiritual leaders are often considered rebels in their time—they are existential threats to the systems in which they live. Imagine our families receiving just as many messages urging us to give as messages to get. Imagine people camping outside stores for days just for the opportunity to donate to a brand new charity. The consumerism that drives our economy will not change overnight, but we can start changing ourselves today.

Spiritual beliefs from around the world place a value on generosity. Buddhism offers one system to codify generosity as a practice of liberation. Judaism emphasizes service for others. In Christian theology, charity (*caritas*) is considered the greatest of virtues. Hinduism, Islam, Jainism, and the Sikh faith all stress the importance of almsgiving, and indigenous traditions across the globe emphasize generosity and community sharing.

But what does generosity really mean? Much of Eastern wisdom describes *dāna* as unconditional giving within our means. Western traditions, too, teach the importance of giving without expectation of gratitude or being paid back, praising anonymity in giving. For example, the Jewish concept of *tzedakah* refers to right and just actions—specifically, donating to others anonymously and offering gifts that promote self-reliance. We should aspire to give without expecting appreciation and applause—something we are particularly unlikely to get as parents.

This idea of generosity also holds true for us, as parents. It means parenting our children how we would want to be parented, speaking to their teachers how we would want them to speak to our child, and driving how we want others to drive when we have our newborn or aging parent in the back seat. It means neither reenacting the imperfect parenting we received nor reacting, rebelling, or rejecting that parenting altogether and spoiling our children. But how do we find the middle path between generosity and obligation, between giving and indulging? We give so much as parents that it's often difficult to discern the difference. Personally, I find it helpful to check in with my intention: am I offering this gift to teach my child, or am I merely trying to get him to stop whining in the checkout line? Most often the answer lies somewhere in between.

reflection How can you tell the difference between true generosity and the kind of giving that isn't helpful? Do you know when you are being generous as opposed to spoiling, feeling obligated, feeling pressure, or even giving more than you can afford, whether financially or emotionally?

The Science of Giving

As we give, our sense of generosity grows stronger, making us more likely to give, and that spreads to those around us like ripples in a pond. Regardless of how you describe this effect (karma, neuroscience, or social psychology), it's a simple matter of cause and effect that you can actually see working in yourself, your family, and the world.

I remember rolling my teenage eyes at a Driver's Ed movie lecturing us that "courtesy is contagious." I rolled my eyes as a jaded adolescent, but it turns out that "social contagions" are real. Ivy League researchers James Fowler and Nicholas Christakis found that acts of kindness and generosity actually do spread from one person to the next. In numerous studies, they demonstrated that merely observing acts of generosity could inspire a ripple effect of "downstream reciprocity" in others up to three degrees of separation.[4] It isn't just that letting a car merge in front of you in traffic will increase the likelihood that the driver will later hold the elevator for someone at the office (and then that next person will be more likely to grab doughnuts for the kids on the way home, who will cuddle with the dog, and so on). Christakis and Fowler also found that just *witnessing* such generosity releases the brain's feel-good chemicals and inspires generosity in others.

Let's look at the biochemistry. Research shows that we get boosts of serotonin (the hormone that regulates mood and anxiety), oxytocin (the "love hormone"), and dopamine (a feel-good neurotransmitter) when we give *and* when we receive. The implications suggest that generosity on either end regulates mood and anxiety and strengthens our immune system; it makes us feel loving *and* loved. We also feel good when we grab our officemate a coffee (getting what my friend Fiona calls "the boy scout buzz"), because we're activating the parts of our brains associated with connection and trust.[5] We also experience an elevation of oxytocin for a few hours, which makes us feel all warm and fuzzy.[6] Oxytocin also blocks cortisol, a stress hormone that has been shown to disrupt growth in children.

All of this means that giving or receiving makes us less likely to snap at our kids, who in turn are less likely to take it out on each other, their classmates, or the family dog. Researchers observe the same endorphins in both the giver and receiver of a gift, though they see a greater amount in the giver.[7] Yet another study asked research subjects to spend five dollars either on themselves or on someone else.[8] To the surprise of the researchers *and* the subjects, those who gave away the five dollars felt better than those who kept the money. Neuroscientist Richard Davidson has spent years researching contemplative practice in Tibetan monks and others. His conclusion? "The best way to activate positive-emotion circuits in the brain is through generosity."[9]

Of course, science and spirituality have their own explanations for the benefits of generosity. The simplest explanation of karma I've heard is that each action we take makes it more likely that we'll perform that same action in the future. Just as we now know that our acts of kindness make us more likely to be generous tomorrow, the opposite is also true: acting in a selfish way today wires us for selfishness tomorrow. However, acting generously also benefits us on a fundamental level: as the more evolved outer cortices of the brain activate and begin to grow, our primitive amygdala calms down (and even shrinks), our heart beats more regularly, our breath flows more evenly, and our blood pressure goes down.

And then there are the long-term benefits of generosity to our well-being and that of our families. There is an old neuroscience adage: "Neurons that fire together, wire together." Each generous action we take rewires the brain for happiness and resilience, one good deed at a time. Positive psychologist Sonja Lyubomirsky found that five generous acts a day can enhance your mood for up to a week.[10] Donating to charity once a month adds as much happiness as a 200 percent raise, and countries with higher levels of charity have higher levels of happiness.[11] Generosity also builds trust between people. It might be common sense that the recipient of generosity feels more trust, but studies also show that the giver's brain regions associated with trust and connection light up,[12] fostering optimism, reducing depression, and creating healthy attachments.[13]

Generosity means action, not abstract platitudes. As researchers have illustrated on psychotherapies of the past, we cannot think our way into a new way of acting; *we have to act our way into a new way of thinking.* This is how our families can become the change we wish to see in the world. If we act generously, the world around us becomes a better place; if we act greedily, it doesn't. Thus, what some call karma may be as simple as science. The Buddhist notion of "as we think and act, so our world becomes" resonates easily with the scientific concept of "neurons that fire together, wire together."

The Importance of Intention

Spiritual traditions don't just place a high value on generous actions; they also focus on the intentions behind generosity—the *why* of our giving. When it comes to generosity, our intention makes all the difference. Sometimes we give for a specific reason—we write thank-you notes and bring gifts to parties, for example. These kinds of gifts help us feel satisfied and teach our kids about social reciprocity.

But sometimes we give with more of an agenda than agreed-upon social graces, as when we expect something back. The lobbyist who provides thousands of dollars in gifts to a politician is looking for a return on his investment. The university benefactor who donates millions likely expects admission for her grandchildren. A parent might offer a son twenty-five dollars for every A he gets. However, as we'll see later, using bribery to change a child's behavior is only buying temporary change and possibly long-term problems.

The more we give with an agenda, the less genuine happiness we can expect for both the giver and the receiver. First of all, when we expect something in return for a gift, we are more likely to become resentful when we don't get it, hurting ourselves and the recipient. Second, acting generously without expecting something in return is what actually triggers the feel-good neurotransmitters. So we always need to look at our intentions. They may be mixed to some extent, but that's okay. If we do things only so others will notice how generous we are or to maintain our identity as generous, or if we expect something in return, the benefits won't materialize on the neurochemical, material, or spiritual level.

When I was in second grade, there was a boy—let's call him Tim—who wanted to be friends with me. During lunch, Tim would offer to trade his cookies for my carrot sticks (quite a bargain in my seven-year-old mind). But when my parents found out about this exchange (in addition to their horror at the junk food), they asked me to reflect on whether the trade was really fair. I knew in my heart it didn't feel right. Tim wanted my friendship, and I wanted his cookies, but I didn't really want to be friends with him, and I doubt that he really wanted those carrots.

How do we give to our children? Are there strings attached? It's not that expectations behind gifts are necessarily a problem—paying for college and expecting our child to study is not unreasonable, for example. However, if we are giving with an agenda, it makes all the difference to be up front and honest about it with ourselves and others—especially our children.

Types of Generosity

Some Eastern philosophy breaks generosity into three categories: gifts of material and wealth, gifts of protection and support, and gifts of wisdom. Ideally, we give what we can, and we give the *best* of what we have: the best material, the best support, and the best wisdom. But the idea isn't to give so much that we cause suffering to ourselves or our family. Give what you can, give what feels right, and then give just a little more. It's like lifting weights or running—we push ourselves in order to meet our goals, but we're careful not to overdo it.

reflection What are some ways you already practice generosity? What are other ways of giving you can try for you and your family?

Gifts of Material and Wealth

Share the wealth, as the saying goes. Material wealth takes various forms—money, gifts, time, and even our bodies (as every mother knows). Even if we're not objectively wealthy, we all have something to give—small amounts of cash, a helping hand to those in need, or volunteering our time. When I was younger, I had little money to offer, but I had plenty of time, physical strength, and energy to give.

We might donate our old things to charity or to friends in need. We also benefit from this by simplifying our lives and decreasing waste of money and stuff. When my wife and I had our first child, we were nearly overwhelmed with the generosity of hand-me-downs from friends and strangers. While they may have been just as thrilled to clear out their basements, there was something magical about being welcomed into this new parent-sharing economy. Gifts took all forms—including itchy and ill-fitting baby clothes, unwanted advice, and soggy green bean casseroles—but they all brought joy to us and meaning to the givers. And as our children get older, we can join the cycle of generosity in a different way by showing our children how to part with old toys and clothes, thereby experiencing the joy of sharing. As they grow up, the stories of the generosity they received when they were young will help shape their outlook on the world and the power of sharing.[14] As we were given, so too we give.

We can also offer the material and wealth of our bodies. Mothers sacrifice their energy and bodies through pregnancy, the birthing process, and breastfeeding. For kids, generosity might mean lending young muscles to carry an aging neighbor's groceries or helping a friend in a pinch. With our bodies we can also give affection through hugs and gentle touch. Even if our bodies don't quite work like they once did, we can all give something.

When you make that gift list for the holidays, consider offering experiences instead of things. Research shows that experiences do more for our happiness and our relationships than objects do.[15] This type of generosity could mean tickets to a show or museum, an art class, or even a vacation. We can also encourage sharing and compassion by giving our children gifts to share, which has the added benefit of the family ending up with less stuff.

reflection   Consider all the gifts your family has been offered over the years—and even over generations. Which of these stories might you share with your children? What are some ways you can add experiences and activities as gifts, in addition to toys?

Gifts of Protection and Support

The second category of generosity refers to protecting others from physical danger or emotional distress. All of us know the sacrifices we'd make if our child were in danger. The same altruistic drive to protect others drives firefighters and psychotherapists, soldiers and social workers, cops and teachers, doctors and nurses, and activists of all stripes. But we don't need to change careers to offer such gifts. We can simply offer an ear to a distraught friend or a shoulder to cry on, smile at a stranger who looks a little down, and teach our children to do the same.

For the longest time, I thought generosity meant dropping change into the hands of a beggar, writing a check to charity, or doing something like helping at a soup kitchen. But when I considered this, I realized these stereotypical "giving" gestures weren't necessarily the *best* of what I had to offer—they weren't what would make the biggest impact. Maybe your hard-earned professional and life experiences are best offered through pro bono consulting to those in need, mentoring a young colleague, or helping out a new parent. The best of what you have might mean sharing your high school basketball skills by coaching your child's team, offering to teach about your job in a classroom, or helping your kid's friends or friend's kids who are struggling.

For me, the best gift of support is a lot like the gift of presence. In my work as a therapist, I share my presence. The work of the therapist is often thought of as giving emotional support and safety. It *is* that, and yet it's much simpler than that. The work of therapists is to share their most authentic, mindful, and compassionate presence to their clients. This gift provides most of the healing. Where else can someone who is sharing from their heart get an uninterrupted hour of absolute attention (on my best days, of course)? When parents are away on business trips or at the gym, teachers are paying attention to other kids, or friends are distracted with drinking, drugs, or digital distractions, kids in therapy (like most kids) long for authentic human connection. So the best I have to offer is compassionate presence, and this makes all the difference when it comes to "success" in therapy. But you don't have to be a therapist to give your presence.

Thich Nhat Hanh suggested that the most precious gift we can offer is our presence: "When mindfulness embraces those we love, they will bloom like flowers."[16] He told a story of a busy, wealthy father who asks what his son wants most for his birthday. The father says, "I can buy you anything in the world, my son." The son responds, "I just want *you*, Daddy." The best of what we have to give is often simply our presence—and that means our *best* presence, not that partial, one-eye-on-the-phone type of attention.

We all are capable of giving our full presence and attention to the people around us. But this can be a tall order in a culture that tells us to give everything to our jobs and our things (particularly our phones), rather than giving our attention to the people we are with. This attention to others means our loved ones, of course, but also strangers in the checkout line or the airplane seat next to us. Of course, the middle path reminds us to give what we can afford. If we don't have time to offer ourselves fully, perhaps that's a sign we should find a way to make time or simply ask for it.

Thich Nhat Hanh also reminds us that sometimes we support those we love by giving them space and time, especially after a conflict. This space offers everyone a chance to heal and grow. In the Zen art of flower arranging, the space that surrounds the flowers is what makes them beautiful. Our children too need space around them to blossom.

Generosity of spirit is another form of support. We can give the benefit of the doubt to a rude stranger who cuts the line, the kid who challenged our own on the playground, or that difficult parent at the parent-teacher organization. If we remember that generosity is the best medicine for anger and resentment toward others, it will help when we have to deal with difficult children, partners, or strangers driving us crazy. Jeff, a client of mine, felt locked in conflict with his daughter. He could see she needed help, but he felt that giving it to her meant surrendering. So we reframed his support as something he was *giving to* his daughter rather than a form of *giving in*. This simple reframe appealed to his best self. Often the people frustrating us are the ones who need our support the most, and they in turn give us opportunities to practice being our best selves through generosity and other values.

reflection   How can you foster the generosity of care and the generosity of spirit in yourself and your family?

Gifts of Wisdom

Perhaps the highest form of generosity is wisdom, which itself gives freedom. You've probably heard the old maxim: "Give someone a fish and you'll feed them for a day; teach them to fish and you'll feed them for a lifetime." This is the gift of wisdom, which we also cultivate in chapter 4. For example, we can use up our energy doing everything for our kids (cooking, cleaning, driving), or we can teach them the skills they will inevitably need for independence (more on this in chapter 5). Teaching them the skills offers not only wisdom but also confidence, self-esteem, and executive function skills.

The gift of wisdom can be hard to identify, as so much of our identity as parents is tied up in the gifts of wealth or support. Still, it's our job as parents not just to tell kids what to do but to also help them find their own paths to wisdom. In turn, they will learn to share with others.

As parents, we may feel perpetually helpless, but each of us has so much wisdom to share with other parents. This wisdom was often acquired the hard way through life's joys and sorrows. Many spiritual teachings suggest that we get back double what we give (on the flip side, this also holds true when we "give" negative things). If we share authentically from our experience as parents, the recipient "gets" that wisdom, and the wisdom doubles in a tangible way. Spiritually speaking, we keep what we have and double it—be it joy or pain, wisdom or bad advice—by giving it away. Each act of generosity brings happiness, wiring neural connections that promote further generosity and wisdom and fostering an environment of exchange and openness in families. In short, our happiness is never lessened by wise and authentic sharing.

reflection   What are some ways you can cultivate the generosity of wisdom in yourself and your family?

Generosity and Discernment

Of course, we have to be careful. We don't want to deplete our emotional or financial stores, and we need to give in a balanced way so that our loved ones and children don't feel neglected, deprived, or jealous. I know many children of dedicated and generous activists or academics who often feel neglected by the gifts their parents shared with the world. It's not just wealthy businesspeople who end up with children longing for their parents' presence. Our own wisdom can help us determine whether we are giving in a way that won't cause more harm elsewhere. Before I became a father, I regularly offered my time to people whenever they asked, but that balance has shifted; I now direct most of my generosity toward my family and myself.

Once we start giving, our brains make it easier to act generously, because we're rewarded with new neural pathways and waves of those wonderful neurotransmitters that make generosity *feel* good. As we've seen, receiving feels good, but *giving* feels even better. Being comforted feels good, but comforting can feel even better. And yet we tend to chase what feels good in order to hold on to that feeling or to get more of it. Although there's nothing wrong with that, at some point, we need to be mindful of our intentions, especially when our ego demands recognition from our largesse.

Giving Too Much and the Challenge of Receiving

One challenge of generosity is making space for others to be generous—toward themselves, toward others, and toward us. We tend to forget this type of generosity when we cling too tightly to our identity as a parent, helper, or giver. Some of us have a habit of giving too much to our relationships, which may enable others in their unhealthy behaviors, like addiction or avoidance. This kind of giving breeds resentment, corrodes relationships, and benefits no one. For example, if you do all the chores around the house while your partner and kids lounge around, at some point you probably resent them for their freedom. What's more, they'll miss out on developing independence or enjoying the satisfaction that comes from doing one's part. Finding a middle way is key.

I recently worked with a high school student named Daniel who was tremendously successful in terms of a college résumé—solid SAT scores, interesting internships, and enviable extracurriculars. But he simply could not make or keep close friends. After a few sessions, he confessed that a group he was hanging out with recently dropped him from their circle, not returning his texts or calls.

"I don't understand," Daniel sighed, slumped on my couch. "I bought them beer every weekend. I always paid for dinner. I gave them rides whenever they asked. I did everything a friend is supposed to do!"

My heart sank. We've all known a kid like this. I didn't know what to say at first; I didn't want to shame him or send the message to not share. After some reflection, I could articulate to him that part of generosity is being generous enough to give our friends space—including the space for equal exchange. Although well intentioned, Daniel was hogging almost all of the generosity, most likely out of fear. Instead of developing friendships, he was fostering discomfort and unwittingly setting the stage to be taken advantage of in the future.

reflection   Consider some ways in which you or someone you know has shared too much, either from fear or from holding too tightly to a particular identity.

Many of us find receiving generosity—be it things, compliments, or wisdom—its own challenge. We unintentionally deny others the opportunity to practice generosity, forgetting that giving benefits both parties. This doesn't mean hitting your friends up for cash while reminding them how good it is for their brain or afterlife. All we need to do is find little ways to receive the generosity of others. Simply asking for help when you need it is an excellent place to begin. I needed a lot of help when my son was born, and I tried to use that opportunity to let go of my identity as a helper and let in the love and assistance of others.

reflection   What do you find more challenging—giving or receiving? Why might that be? In what ways does it matter who the person is? How might shifting the balance between giving and receiving change things in your life?

Finding and Creating Opportunities to Give

In many spiritual traditions, giving is *built in*. Adherents tithe, practice almsgiving, or pass a basket through the congregation. In much of Asia, monks quietly go on begging rounds through the village or city, bowls in hand, to be fed by locals or to receive premade care packages full of snacks, soaps, and robes. These cultures have evolved to include rituals of generosity that sustain their spiritual leaders, while offering opportunities for laypeople to reap the benefits of giving.

Conversely, our culture has evolved to encourage "frictionless" consumption, making it easier than ever to buy things we don't want or need. We can still find opportunities to practice generosity, but where do we start? Think of the sun: it shines in all directions—up and down, inward and outward, near and far. Generosity practice can be like that, too.

You can start with yourself. Find a small way to extend generosity to yourself. As you wait for your kids after school or stand at the sink to wash dishes, try saying a kind word to yourself. You could also thank or compliment yourself—or even just give yourself a break. Consider the three types of generosity—material, comfort, and wisdom. Buy yourself a comfy sweatshirt, put a little cash in your retirement fund, reach out for help when you need to, read an inspiring poem, or spend time with a spiritual teacher. The opportunities are endless.

But watch out for getting self-care and self-indulgence mixed up. Those less-than-healthy practices of overeating, overdrinking, and overindulgence are different from preparing a special meal, enjoying a glass of your favorite wine, or purchasing the occasional treat. On the flip side, we can also give ourselves a hard time for taking needed breaks, labeling necessary rests as self-indulgence.

reflection   What is one generous thing you can do for yourself right now? What would it take for you to stop reading right now and do it?

Just as the sun shines outward to touch all the objects closest to it first, try extending generosity toward those closest to you. Take your partner out to dinner, give your friend a hug, or tell your child something you appreciate about her. Text an authentic compliment to a friend or thank someone for buying you this book (or recommending it). Try it, *right now*! Notice how you feel—before, during, and after. Commit to this practice with a friend for a week or so, and check in with each other about it as you go.

The ancient philosopher Epictetus instructed, "Never suppress a generous impulse."[17] The Buddha advised his followers to avoid acting when feeling greedy, but instead to wait on action until a generous impulse arises. Today, the Buddhist teacher Sylvia Boorstein prescribes five unplanned acts of generosity a day. Although generosity is more of an *action* than a contemplation, it may be helpful at the end of your day to reflect on opportunities for generosity or when others were unexpectedly generous with you. In turn, you can share these with your family and reflect with them about what you are doing.

After you have offered generosity to yourself and to someone close to you, try giving it to a stranger. Take a moment to contemplate what that might look like, knowing there's joy even in just contemplating an act of generosity. What would it be like to write a small check to a charity you've never given to before? To treat the person behind you in line to a cup of coffee? To feed a stranger's parking meter? Maybe it's looking the checkout clerk in the eyes and asking how she is doing, wishing her a good day *and meaning it*. Maybe it means reaching out to someone you don't know in your parents' circle and offering support. You might even do something kind for someone who frustrates you. A friend of mine (who happens to be an atheist Twelve-Stepping Muslim) has a simple practice of letting people in front of her take left turns at stoplights (if you know what the traffic is like around Cambridge, this qualifies for an incredible rebirth, afterlife, or sainthood—whatever your belief system is). You can also consider such generosity of spirit toward those difficult people in your life when it's wise to do so.

Encouraging Generosity in Our Families

As every parent knows, teaching kids to share is a tall order. Two-year-olds actually prefer giving to getting but then relapse, struggling with sharing until they're older.[18] But this too offers an opportunity to practice patience and generosity of spirit.

As children get older, research shows that even a minor shift in the language we use makes all the difference in encouraging sharing.[19] Instead of telling your children that "sharing is a nice thing to do," you can let them know that "nice people share," helping them cultivate a healthy identity as a generous person, without becoming like my lonely patient Daniel or my cookie-trading classmate from second grade. We can also encourage family sharing and connection by shifting our language to saying things like "the car" rather than "my car," which is a practice that correlates with family stability.

Angela Duckworth, the author of *Grit: Passion, Perseverance, and the Science of Success*, has a family policy in which everyone practices one hard thing every day that they want to get better at—Angela practices yoga, her husband runs, and her kids do ballet and play the piano. I'll discuss this idea more in chapter 8, but for now let's build on Angela's practice. Imagine having everyone in the family engage in one generous or kind activity that matters to them. What could this mean? When children are younger, generosity might mean noticing and following up on opportunities for simple acts of kindness on a daily basis—inviting over the new kid or holding the door open for a stranger. Some kids can choose a "secret friend" to watch out for throughout the school year or a neighbor they help with yard work. Many schools pair up older children to read to kids in younger grades; some even have the older kids teach mindfulness to the little ones. What matters is finding activities that are meaningful to them.

As parents, we can model generosity by baking cookies for kids to share at school, donating used books to an underfunded library or prison, or giving old toys to needy kids for the holidays. If you regularly donate gifts or money to charity, letting your kids drop a dollar in the basket, hand off the cans to the food bank staff, or place clothes into the donation bin at the thrift store will be satisfying and memorable. One friend has a family tradition of giving money to kids for holidays and their birthdays in the following form: fifty dollars in cash and a fifty dollar check to a charity of the child's choice. Other families give kids three jars for their allowance: one for spending, one for saving, and another for sharing (or three-chambered piggy banks that do the same). This tradition instructs kids in the value of generosity while simultaneously teaching them how to make wise choices. Involving your kids in decisions about family donations can be another way to share generosity and clarify your family's values.

As kids enter adolescence, community service is often a school requirement, but we often forget to make that service personally meaningful. For example, kids with an interest in the outdoors can clear trails or help maintain parks or beaches. Budding creatives can sing, perform, tell stories, put on an art exhibit, or paint a mural at a school, hospital, or retirement community. If performing isn't their thing, they can volunteer at an art museum, community theater, library, or dedicated creative space (where there is often a shortage of funding and staff). If your children enjoy academics, they can share their skills with younger or less privileged kids. If they love cooking, perhaps they can prepare a meal at a local shelter or deliver meals to the home-bound. Young fashionistas or antiquarians can help at a charity thrift store. For kids with passionate feelings about a political, social, or even personal cause, many campaigns offer ways for them to get involved. Young athletes might referee or coach younger kids. Computer skills can be put to good work at a cause they care about or simply by teaching senior citizens how to use their new phone. And don't just send your kids out by themselves; you can join them on these generosity adventures or take them with you on your own.

reflection   What are simple acts of generosity you and your family can perform from time to time?

Generosity and Generativity

Generosity is intimately tied in with the other paramis; it's difficult to talk about one virtue without referring to the others. Generosity relates to ethics, because giving is the opposite of taking more than we need. Generosity also requires wisdom, of course, and giving wisdom is considered the highest form of generosity. Giving is also an act of renunciation that requires patience. And it's impossible to discuss generosity without seeing it through the lens of kindness.

But the biggest gift we offer our children is a secure and loving family. If we provide them with a safe, securely attached upbringing, that in itself creates conditions for children to thrive in work and love and to be generous later on in life.[20] How you raise your child is a gift not only to them but also to the world. Remember too that generosity is generative. It creates positive feelings and benefits for us and for those around us, and it becomes easier the more we practice. When we practice giving, we create a habit, rewiring ourselves to make giving a reflex—as opposed to something we have to remind ourselves to do with great effort.

Both science and wisdom traditions promise that the more we share—be it stuff, protection, or wisdom—the more we receive in return. What we give is less important than the intention behind the act of giving. Generosity opens our heart and connects us with others. In this way, it helps dissolve the divisions between self and other and radiates lovingkindness out into widening circles.

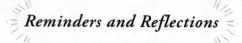

Reminders and Reflections

- According to the most recent research, generosity cultivates health and happiness in both the giver and the receiver.

- People with more self-control tend to act more generously, and thinking about others can increase self-control.

- Generosity means not only money and material things but also emotional support and wisdom.

- What types of generosity has your family received over the years?

- What do you think is the difference between generosity and obligation? Between generosity and overindulgence?

- How do you feel after you give? How does that feeling differ from what you felt before you shared?

- Practice generosity as a family by talking about opportunities for giving things, time, effort, and wisdom in creative ways.

- When buying gifts, don't forget to offer experiences like museum passes and tickets to performances, as these lead to more happiness and cherished memories than mere things.

- Teach kids to give early in their lives by including money for charity in allowance and gifts.

- Help your teens find community service options that don't just fulfill required hours but are also meaningful to them.

- Catch your kids in the act. Let them know that you see and value their generosity when you witness it. Give them space—don't hurry them along when you see they are helping others.

CHAPTER 2

why doing the right thing
is the right thing to do

(Raising Ethics—Śīla)

Lessons in ethics and morality may not have been what you had in mind when you picked up this book. Even the phrase "family values" smacks of hypocrisy. And if you are anything like me, you might think, "I'm already ethical! I drive an environmentally friendly car (when I have to drive at all), I recycle, I practice nonviolence and honesty, and I'm generally a do-gooder. What more do I need to learn about ethics?" Well, personally, the more deeply I have studied this issue, the more important and nuanced I've found ethics to be.

To start, what we're calling ethics are simply guidelines that promote everyone's safety and well-being. The Indian term for ethics is *śīla*, which means "cool and peaceful," like a tree that shelters everyone with its shade. So, ethics in this context is about protecting ourselves, our families, our communities, and our planet. Think about it—when people feel safe, they are far less likely to misbehave or harm others physically or emotionally. When we protect others, we protect ourselves and our families in the process. Likewise, when we skillfully protect ourselves and our families through ethical behavior, we protect others.

Ethical behavior allows us to live in harmony with ourselves, our families, and our communities. For ourselves, when our actions match our words, we live with integrity and without the discomfort of cognitive dissonance. Harmony in our families means we understand and take care of each other. And when we agree on and follow the rules of our community, we know where we stand and can feel safe. Ethical living means we offer everyone safety, comfort, and protection. When we apply wisdom to ethics, we begin to understand how we are all interconnected, that harming others harms us, and how acting skillfully becomes more clear and straightforward. We could also call this karma or just simple common sense.

We can also think of ethics like a guardrail that helps us know where the edge is; it's a barrier that keeps us from going over the brink when we get too close. With our children, this might take the form of clear and consistent boundaries, which are key in raising resilient, thriving children. But I'm astonished at how many parents (myself included) have trouble with this idea; instead, we regularly overreact or underreact to our kids' behavior. We might tell our kids to calm down before making a major decision, even as we forget to calm down before doling out a consequence to our kids. This confuses kids even more when we make threats that we clearly won't follow through with ("We're getting rid of the dog if you don't walk it!") or have to walk back similarly huge consequences for minor transgressions because they occurred on *our* bad day. Every one of us can get caught off guard, but we can also learn to better recognize when our own emotional buttons are pushed. Or we can take a break and tell the kids we need to think things over and talk things through, thus saving effort in the long run. Doing so also promotes consistency, feelings of safety, and a whole lot less regret.

Ethics isn't just about concepts or words. Like the values covered in the rest of this book, ethics is about getting off your cushion and living those principles as a family. That means doing what's right, not just avoiding what's wrong. Here's a helpful formula for ethical action: first, ask if a particular action will hurt others; then, ask if it will help others. If the answer is unclear, check in with your intuition—your "gut."

The Five Precepts

All spiritual and wisdom traditions come with commandments, laws, or guidelines, though these might vary in details and incentives—the afterlife, blessings for future generations, a higher rebirth, or better physical and mental health. Buddhism has five precepts that overlap with most other spiritual traditions; these precepts are meant as aspirations to be followed as opposed to commandments. They are more about guidance than governance. Similarly, we want our children to develop their own inner moral compass. In the end, we want them to do the least harm to themselves and others in this already dangerous world and to move in the direction of healing it.

Each precept entails a proscriptive side (unskillful actions to refrain from) and a prescriptive side (skillful and wholesome thoughts, words, and deeds to perform).

1. Don't kill or hurt living creatures. Support and protect life.

2. Don't steal or take things that aren't offered. Only take what you need, and always give your fair share.

3. Don't lie, gossip, or mislead people. Speak gently, speak the truth, and speak important truths.

4. Don't abuse or harmfully indulge in your sexual energy. Use it wisely, kindly, and generously to create joy and connection.

5. Don't become intoxicated. Nourish yourself in ways that cultivate clarity and wisdom.

Again, the idea is not for these precepts to be rules that we will invariably fall short of, but aspirations to be our best. The reality is that we don't always know in each moment what to do or how to be our best, but if we can decide from our best self in that moment, then the outcome is likely to be a good one for us and those around us. Consider the cultivation metaphor: some seeds will blossom on their own, but to thrive, many plants need to grow on a structure like a trellis. That trellis is precisely what the precepts provide.

Let's look at each one in a bit more depth.

1. Don't kill or hurt living creatures.
Support and protect life.

It's no surprise that this precept comes first. Even though most of us probably aren't out there wantonly harming others, we should bear in mind that this precept refers to refraining from violence not just in action but also in speech and thought. This includes when we consciously or unconsciously perpetuate emotional violence.

Supporting and protecting life includes supporting the well-being of our ecosystem and planet. There are many ways to teach our children that life is sacred. We might help them care for a pet or garden or encourage them to not stomp on ants or wantonly yank petals off flowers. I can still remember a tree in my grand-parents' yard. It was perfect for climbing, but it required me to stand atop a milk crate to reach the lowest branch. So I asked my grandfather if I could hammer some wood into the trunk to make a ladder. He patiently pointed out that it would hurt the tree and that it would take only a little bit more effort on my part to use the milk crate to reach those first branches. I would not have given hurting the tree a second thought had my grandfather not taken the time to talk with me about it.

When we first learn these precepts, questions often arise—for example, "Can I kill the ants in my house?" We can ponder questions like these forever, but a wiser use of our energy is to maintain a clean house so that ants will keep away in the first place. Part of ethical behavior is creating the conditions under which such dilemmas are less likely to arise.

I hope it goes without saying that following precepts like these ideally involves right action without self-righteousness. I remember a woman smugly asking Thich Nhat Hanh, "Shouldn't we all be vegans?" He paused, smiled patiently, and suggested that the woman do what is best for her, keeping in mind that absolute attachment to the precepts can generate more suffering for us and others. He also pointed out that if we carry the logic too far, we couldn't eat steamed vegetables, because doing so would mean killing bacteria and the vegetables themselves. What I heard was another reminder to challenge ourselves to do our best, while aiming for a reasonable middle path.

Many families have grown concerned about the epidemic of bullying. Growing up, I and many of my friends were the children of peace activists and were admonished against physical aggression. And yet, we experienced (and engaged in) frequent "relational bullying"—a term that didn't exist at the time. Even while I was staunchly opposed to physical violence, I look back and cringe at the psychological cruelty I inflicted on others, not realizing the impact at the time. Sticks and stones may break our bones, but being excluded or called names actually hits the same pain receptors as physical pain. This is true whether people are bullied in person or online. We may think that *our* kids would never be unkind, but consider that studies find that meanness and appearance are the best predictors of popularity in teenage girls. In teen boys, these predictors are substance abuse and an objectifying attitude toward women.[1]

Although humans can be aggressive, we don't need to fear such feelings. It may actually be healthier to examine them more closely. In one surprising study, preschoolers who played aggressively with their toys by themselves were actually less aggressive with peers, perhaps because they practiced regulating their aggressive impulses.[2] If your child's play concerns you, take a page from play therapists. Join children in their world, get curious about the characters in their storyline, find out why they are aggressive, and brainstorm other ways they could resolve their differences. When it comes to aggressive physical play, some experts believe that safe roughhousing can help kids build better social and executive function skills.[3] I detested roughhousing and wrestling as a child, but as a father, I've been surprised at how much my own son enjoys the close physical contact that comes with rolling around on the floor together. I've found this activity a wonderful opportunity to feel physical closeness, have fun, laugh, and practice being both loving and careful.

reflection   When do you and your family tend to respond with aggression in thought, speech, and behavior? What are your family's values about physically and emotionally aggressive play? How does your family differentiate aggression (and violence) from playing or joking around, whether physically or verbally?

2. Don't steal or take things that aren't offered. Only take what you need, and always give your fair share.

While chapter 7 will examine honesty more closely, let's take a quick look here at some of the ways we might take things from others that aren't freely offered. Although we may not be raiding our children's piggy bank or college fund, we might unconsciously take from them by undermining their independence, self-esteem, and confidence. We might also take from their time, affection, energy, and care in ways we don't always realize. We could also investigate how we take what is not freely offered from our spouse or even ourselves.

We can expand this reflection, of course, to consider our local and global community. Do the resources we use come to us fairly? Are we contributing our fair share to our communities by paying our taxes honestly and showing up to city council and PTO meetings? Research also reveals that we are more likely to bend the rules if doing so benefits our families.[4] Thus, we should consider what message we're sending our children when we ask for special treatment or otherwise game the system on their behalf.

3. Don't lie, gossip, or mislead people. Speak gently, speak the truth, and speak important truths.

As above, we'll look at this precept more in chapter 7. I do think it's important to bear in mind that "right" speech in this context also means "effective" speech. I believe that the guidelines for practicing healthy speech serve that purpose. The Buddha suggested that before we speak we should reflect on whether what we are about to say is true, kind, gentle, and timely. Here, I've adapted the popular acronym **THINK** (before you speak) with some slight variations:

Is it **t**rue?

Is it **h**elpful?

Am **I** the one to say it?

Is it **n**ecessary, **n**ow?

Is it **k**ind?

Is it true? First and foremost, we want to speak *the* truth whenever possible to avoid harming ourselves or others. Lying usually comes from an attempt to defend our self-image and identity, or ego, which only causes more suffering. At a more nuanced level, we want to speak important truths that help others.

Is it helpful? We may want to reflect on what we are about to say and determine whether it will actually be of benefit. When we gossip or offer certain kinds of feedback to those we love (or don't), the words we choose might very well be true, but they might not exactly be helpful.

Am I the one to say it? Some statements may be true and helpful, but they also may be none of our business. As a therapist, I often *am* the one to say it, but in other roles in my life, I'm not. Gentle feedback might be better received from a coach than from a parent, and I'm certainly not going to be the one to teach my son calculus. On the other hand, I am often the best person in the family to explain something emotionally challenging or to break bad news to my child.

Is it necessary, now? Even when the above criteria are met, we can ask ourselves if what we want to say is actually *necessary*. Sometimes we speak just to fill the space or alleviate our anxiety with chatter. In my training as a therapist, I learned to use the acronym WAIT (Why Am I Talking?) before I would speak. When we don't first stop to think, we can inhibit a moment of budding insight or put our words in someone's mouth or even just say something entirely unnecessary. Silence can offer rare opportunities for intimate moments, especially when we're just listening, rather than waiting for our turn to speak.

One of my own habits I'm trying to break is gossip. Talking about others might involve truth, but rarely is it necessary. Bragging is also often true but not exactly needed, and it is almost always annoying. "N" also stands for *now*—keep in mind that timing is everything.

Is it kind? The old adage "if you don't have anything nice to say, don't say anything at all" fits nicely here. Most people, especially children, are likely to be most receptive to new ideas when they are explained patiently and kindly. Adolescents often default to negativity rather than kindness when trying to connect. It can be a lot easier to agree that something (or someone) is "lame" than to take a risk and suggest that something is "cool" or interesting. We adults are not always more evolved or mature in this regard.

Practicing or teaching the **THINK** guidelines in speech can prove challenging, but doing so is surprisingly effective. Right speech also means effective speech, and I believe these guidelines can help us all be effective communicators when we honor all the concepts. Following this **THINK** practice can also bring some interesting discoveries. For example, how much do we really *have* to say? Imagine if these were the rules for political debates?

reflection How much of your speech involves talking about other people? In conversation, how much do you connect with others around positive things (as opposed to negative topics or comments)? Which of these five **THINK** guidelines do you and your family find most challenging?

4. Don't abuse or harmfully indulge in your sexual energy. Use it wisely, kindly, and generously to create connection and joy.

Of all the precepts, this may be the one that's the most difficult to talk about, especially since many of us live with shame or even trauma about sexuality. We may also struggle to find common ground with our children as they discover and assert their sexual preferences and identities, even as social norms undergo rapid change. Factoring in the variety of familial, religious, and social norms, the rules and expectations around our sexuality add a lot of emotional charge to what constitutes "best use" of our powerful sexual energies.

Let's begin by looking at some of the most obvious illustrations of what's considered sexual misconduct. For parents, misusing sexual energy often means acting outside of the agreements of our relationship. Doing so may result in instability, mistrust, anger, and sadness in our family.

Sexual misconduct not only hurts families; it can also wound entire communities. In my own church growing up, I saw the damage committed by my own priest firsthand. This type of misconduct harms individuals while also sending out ripples of suspicion, shame, and confusion into the larger community. Such behavior has damaged and destroyed countless spiritual communities of every stripe.

Of course, there are other less damaging day-to-day examples of the misuse of sexual energy. While working at a teen retreat a few years ago, Charlie, one of the older teens, admitted that he would often start flirting with someone he found physically attractive before actually getting to know them. "I'm not seeing them as a whole person; just as an object," Charlie confessed. "And I'm probably not showing my most authentic self either, but showing what I think they want to see." How many of us adults can admit to the same behavior with Charlie's honesty? Even as adults, we may unconsciously flirt with colleagues or others in our lives. Well before it crosses a relational boundary, this type of behavior can distract us from authentic connection with that person, as well as with our family.

We want to teach our kids about sex in a positive way at the right time, rather than keeping the topic shrouded in secrecy or shame. But these days, the right time may come earlier than we might expect. In the age of the Internet, kids typically get exposed to pornography around age eleven. How many of us would rather our kids learn about sexuality from *anywhere* but pornography? As adults, our job is to teach children not only the physical aspects of sex, but the personal and emotional ones as well. As they get older, we can explain the social and political aspects of sex and how sexuality is misused to shame, control, or scapegoat people. Thankfully, the younger generation seems to have an easier time discussing all of this than many of us do.

Teaching Children about Consent and Boundaries

Consent might be the most important aspect of sexuality we can teach our children. Studies indicate that one in four women on college campuses experiences some form of sexual assault, and far more experience assault within their lifetime.[5] Men, too, bear the shame and stigma of having been assaulted. Worse, our culture tends to minimize and deny sexual assault, while blaming those who do come forward. Although this culture of shame and cover-up is slowly moving toward a healthier culture of affirmative consent, we still have a long way to go. The challenge comes in teaching young people about consent and boundaries—not in a shaming and frightening way, but in an open, empowering, and sex-positive way.

These conversations are not easy. However, part of *right* speech means talking openly and plainly about sex, sexuality, and consent. For some of us, this may be as uncomfortable as it is for our kids, often due to our own histories. But it may also be an opportunity to educate ourselves alongside our children, to stop passing shame and confusion to the next generation, and to remind us all that sex is a normal and pleasurable part of life.

The younger we can start teaching our children about consent in nonsexual behavior, the more likely they will carry such an understanding into sexual behavior as they become sexually aware and active. Children as young as three or four can begin to understand that not saying no isn't the same as saying yes. (The Good Men Project has an excellent article about teaching kids consent, which inspired some of the ideas here.[6]) We can also teach our children to respect when playmates say no or want to stop playing, as well as empowering them to say "no" or "stop" in all kinds of other situations. Likewise, we can teach and model that "yes means yes" in different types of play by checking in with them before, during, and after games. Of course, we can include ourselves in that circle of consent, asking and respecting our kids when they really want us to stop tickling or when roughhousing isn't fun anymore. We adults can even practice taking time-outs ourselves.

Parents, teachers, and childcare workers can also explain nonverbal cues. For example, if your child's friend says she is having fun but looks overwhelmed or tired, you can help your child see the mismatch between those two messages. This is an important emotional intelligence skill in any situation, of course, but it becomes especially important when playing with younger kids, new kids, or kids with less power.

When we model saying "no" and meaning it, we are setting firm, consistent boundaries. When we model accepting "stop" for an answer, we model empowerment and show that saying "no" is not only okay but also normal. This modeling teaches our children that everyone has permission to stop and remove consent when they feel like it. It also teaches them patience, respecting other people's boundaries, and being comfortable with setting their own. We want to remind kids that choices about their body are theirs, just as other people's bodies belong to themselves.

When we use this proactive (rather than reactive) approach, we can help kids pause and be less impulsive in all of their behavior. This approach also offers nonshaming lessons in healthy boundaries and communication.

Talking to Children about Sex

If our kids feel shameful talking about sex, they may find it even more difficult to ask appropriate questions. Shame can also make it harder when teens do become sexually active to hear what someone else is asking for, to ask for what they want or don't want with a future partner, or to report sexual misconduct. By making sex difficult to talk about in our culture, we create conditions not only for unfulfilling experiences but also for actual violations. One tragedy of our patriarchal system is the lack of transparency and justice for survivors of sexual assault. Young people often feel afraid to share a bad experience due to stigma, shame, or fear. To make matters worse, when survivors do open up about their experiences, families and friendships can be torn apart as people take sides or are unsupportive. I've worked with survivors and their families for years (as well as with perpetrators and their families), and I've witnessed so many kinds of suffering from sexual misconduct as it ripples outward.

Even before kids become sexually active or curious, we can demystify sex by talking about it in basic physical and emotional terms. When we demystify sex, we destigmatize it. By doing so, we remove the shame and empower kids to understand their own bodies. Kids can become more aware of what feels good to them and what doesn't, even in non-sexual ways. From there, they can understand the relationship between physical and emotional feelings.

As children explore their bodies as toddlers, use anatomical language rather than nicknames when referring to their genitals. Kids should also learn the functions of their different body parts. Ideally, they do this by looking through books or talking with you or a pediatrician about it. In this way, they also learn where to get accurate information the next time they are curious, rather than looking into questionable sources online or elsewhere.

As we have more frank sex talks with our children into middle school, we lay the groundwork for discussing affirmative consent in "yes means yes" terms in an extension of childhood play norms. On top of that, the mechanics of sex are already understood, and hopefully we are now *all* feeling more comfortable with the conversation. At this point, it might be time to talk with your children about birth control and protection from sexually transmitted infections (STIs), as well as the emotional aspects of sexual activity.

In addition, it's important to expose children to diverse models of beauty and relationships, as well as a range of models of masculinity and femininity. As adolescence approaches, we might listen to the language kids use to talk about their own bodies and those of other people in respectful ways, encouraging them to see beyond objectification. When our kids express an interest (friendship or otherwise) in others, we can discuss and ask about what nonphysical attributes are also attractive—for example, sense of humor, athletic skill, or intellectual prowess. I vividly remember the moment in middle school when my friends were referring to girls in our grade as "bitches." I actually wondered, *Are they serious, or are they just imitating the music we listen to?* In retrospect, it didn't matter; it was still objectifying. I didn't speak up then, but I wish someone had told me that doing so would have been okay and that I probably wasn't the only one feeling uncomfortable in that room.

Although these conversations can be difficult, families that avoid them tend to have kids with higher rates of unplanned pregnancies, STIs, and possibly even sexual assault. In other words, those few minutes of discomfort will be worth it. Not only will we encourage our children to be happier and safer, we'll also help create a safer and more enlightened world for future generations.

reflection What values did you grow up with around sexuality? What did you learn about sexual ethics and consent from family, adults, or society? How have these messages changed, and what might you pass on (or not pass on) to your family? What would you want your grown children to understand about sexual ethics?

5. Don't become intoxicated. Nourish yourself in ways that cultivate clarity and wisdom.

This precept might seem obvious when it comes to caring for our children. We are far more likely to put our families in danger and to screw up the other precepts if we are intoxicated. Alcohol and drugs take time, money, and presence away from our families, as I see all the time in my work. To make matters worse, when we use intoxicants, we encourage others around us to do so. Even if those around us are not using, they may become clouded by the strong emotional reactions of confusion, fear, and denial that our intoxication can cause.

When we become parents, we may need to change our behaviors and habits and respectfully encourage others to do so as well. My parents and many of their generation cite us (their children) as the reason they quit smoking. That was beneficial for our parents, of course, but it also had a positive influence on our generation. For some of us, there may be difficult conversations with relatives around their substance use. My wife and I had to confront our relatives about their level of drinking (which occasionally begins in the morning)—not just for our child's physical safety, but also because of the message it communicates to the rest of us about how much our in-laws want to be present.

Of course, this precept doesn't just refer to alcohol and drugs. Spiritual teachers remind us that various types of consumption can also cloud the mind. The media we watch, the music we listen to, and the company we keep can all affect our views on violence, sex and sexuality, and substance use, as well as honesty and the other values addressed in this book. I'm sure we've all seen children become more aggressive after playing certain games or watching particular movies. I even notice how my driving changes when I listen to angry music. If we adults find ourselves changed by music or video games, imagine how that rewires a young brain.

One of the most influential studies on media violence was Albert Bandura's infamous "Bobo experiment," which resulted in children violently attacking an inflatable clown doll after watching videos of adults (or even cartoons) doing the same.[7] The kids whacked the doll at twice the rate of those children who did not see the video, and some even attacked a live person dressed as clown! As most parents know, children learn more by what we do than what we say. Thus, the point is not to label media (or other substances) as inherently good or bad, but to be mindful of what we do and how we talk about it with our kids. Search out television programs that show far more acts of kindness than violence or video games that encourage cooperation, and talk about what you watch, play, and read.

PRACTICE Mindful Music

One of my favorite activities with kids is to play happy music, sad music, silly music, and angry music. We carefully listen to each type and notice the feelings in our bodies and minds. We also pay attention to how the music changes our impulses.

Kids and Substances

As a therapist, I regularly deal with the topic of kids and drugs. My internal gauge on substances may be off because of my own history with substances. I struggled with drugs as a young man until my early twenties, when I decided to take a route of abstinence and recovery. That being said, I know plenty of kids who experiment with drugs without endangering themselves emotionally, legally, or physically. But using substances undeniably raises these risks. The most important thing, in my experience, is to speak plainly and honestly with children about the risks of using substances.

When my kids are old enough, we will explain to them our family's difficulties with addiction and how they relate to our family's current values. I will also present the latest understanding of addiction, that it emerges from three factors: genetics, psychological experiences, and exposure. As parents, we only have some influence over two of these factors. But I've found kids surprisingly receptive to the knowledge that the earlier someone begins using drugs, the worse the impact on brain and emotional development and the higher the likelihood of addiction. This also holds true for alcohol, pornography, gambling, screen time, or any other behaviors that can become compulsive. The good news about a young brain is it can learn and adapt quickly; the bad news is that it can become more easily wired for addiction.

But here, too, perhaps a middle path is preferred. Amish and Mennonite communities that practice the *Rumspringa* rite of passage might be on to something. Their young adults go to live outside of their traditional community, which often involves a year or two of decadence; most of those kids then return to the fold and resume the spiritual path of their upbringing.[8] Perhaps the U.S. college system is not so different, which may be why gap years or time off for kids to "get it out of their system" (or simply let their prefrontal lobes develop) before they step into the responsibilities of adulthood can be so positive.

In various spiritual traditions, substances play every role from sin to sacrament. The precepts and many spiritual traditions are fairly explicit on this front, though many on the spiritual path are far from teetotalers—often infamously so. Perhaps with substances, as with everything, it makes the most sense to aim for the middle path. Even when right and wrong are not so clear externally, we can look inward to discover what is right for us. With substances, that answer is clearly different for each of us. Likewise, we want our children to learn their limits and what is right for them, but we also want to make sure they don't become another statistic of alcohol poisoning at college or another casualty of the drug epidemic.

If you do worry about your family, I find a few questions useful when assessing substance use that also help kids reflect on why they are using. For starters, one of the best predictors of how much kids are using is to ask how much their friends use. I also ask how they would know whether a friend is using too often or too much and what their plan is for those situations. I encourage kids to reflect on ways their friends' behaviors change under the influence in terms of judgment, coordination, aggression, and reading social and sexual cues. I also ask how it affects their friends' values. I then ask kids to reflect on these questions for themselves. I try to get curious about what they like and don't like about using, and I invite them to consider what other activities might give them the same feelings they gain from using but without the associated risks.

I also worry about kids with very high tolerances. Depending on their current level of safety, I may not lead right away by telling them to stop altogether. Instead, I'll suggest that they try stopping for a week or two to notice what happens. If that's too hard for them, I'll suggest going to a party but not drinking *right away*; instead, I ask them to notice what those five minutes (or one or two) are like before they grab a beer, take a shot, or hit the vape. If that's all they can do, we talk about the discomfort in those minutes of sobriety. Doing so reveals quite a bit about why kids use and the degree to which they feel they are in control. Of course, I also always urge kids to use a designated driver, but I go one step further—I encourage them to have a designated sober person who can retain sound judgment in the event of a bad situation.

reflection What are your experiences and values as they relate to drugs and alcohol? Have they changed since becoming a parent? What do you consider healthy experimentation, and what do you consider dangerous use for yourself and your kids? How do you think you and your partner will respond to your child's experimentation? What models do you and your kids have for moderation?

At some point in Mahatma Gandhi's life, a mother brought her son to see him about her son's affinity for sweets. "Will you please tell my son to stop eating so many sweets?" she begged. Gandhi listened, reflected, and politely asked her to return in two weeks. In the meantime, the son continued to eat his sweets, and the mother fumed the entire time, right up until they returned. This time Gandhi looked the young boy in the eyes and said, "Son, those sweets will rot your teeth, and you should stop eating them at once." The boy nodded and told the master he would do his best. The mother leaned in and asked, "Why did I have to wait two weeks for that?" The old man smiled. "Well, you see, it took me all of the last two weeks to break the habit myself." To me, this story demonstrates the importance of showing—not telling—our children the way.

Staying on Track

We live with happiness, integrity, and internal harmony when our beliefs, words, and actions line up. However, when how we think, speak, and act don't align, we experience what psychologists call *cognitive dissonance*.

This discomfort puts pressure on our unconscious minds to come back into balance—we either unconsciously try to get caught (think of all the scandals involving righteous politicians and religious leaders) or create mental justifications for the dissonance, which then becomes a slippery slope toward more unethical behavior. When we act unethically or immorally, it also damages us psychologically. Researchers call this *moral injury*—a condition related to the post-traumatic stress disorder (PTSD) that perpetrators of violence and trauma experience.

As humans, we all make mistakes, often even in front of our families. When this happens, we should own it with our kids, so they can learn to own it themselves. I've worked with many families who wonder why their kids don't apologize or take responsibility for their actions, when the parents rarely embody these behaviors themselves. Other parents try to avoid arguing in front of their kids; although that may be wise, parents' fighting is not itself a problem for kids—it's the type of fighting and whether parents can model the repair and apologies afterward.

reflection   Which of the five precepts in this chapter would you find hardest to practice in your own life or with your family? Which is the most difficult to talk openly about with your children? Do you find it hard to model mistakes and repairs in front of your family?

Even in challenging times, we can create the conditions under which we and our families are most likely to act ethically. Studies show that in a psychological principle known as *ego depletion*, we are more likely to slide ethically when our prefrontal cortex is short on glucose from exhaustion in some way.[9] Simply put, when we practice self-care through rest, healthy living, and stress management, we are likely to be at our best. Remembering to HALT (checking to see if we are hungry, angry, anxious, lonely, or tired) can help. We can also be mindful of situations in which we are more likely to act out, particularly anonymous situations like driving, posting comments online, or even wearing helmets in sports or costumes at Halloween. This is why the fifth precept is so important.

Explicit or subtle reminders of ethical behaviors can serve a purpose. Adherents of many spiritual traditions wear particular clothing or jewelry to remind them of their values, from hats to beads to under-garments. A particular park in Japan had a significant litter problem for years, and signs forbidding litter didn't seem to help. However, when the park managers placed Shinto symbols around, littering was reduced significantly in an effect that was dubbed "divine prevention."[10] While I'm not advocating putting religious icons around in public, posting symbolic reminders that work for you and your family might be worth considering, such as artwork that symbolizes your family's values or a photo of a teacher or relative who embodies ethics.

The Middle Path

When writing a book about values, it's a challenge to not be too per-fectionistic, literal, or self-righteous. No one enjoys the ethical nag, the self-righteous scold, or the pious Pollyanna. We know we can't be perfectly ethical at every moment; however, it also doesn't help to ignore the issue altogether. We have to form some positive relation-ship with the prescriptive side of ethics without clinging too tightly to the issue. Our sense of ethics works like a muscle—we can strengthen it with practice, but we can also wear it out from overexertion. Perhaps this is why we see so many supposed exemplars of ethics fall from grace. Studies have even found that ethicists themselves are less ethical than the general population![11]

A friend of mine worked at an ultraprogressive school for gifted chil-dren, a safe space for kids who had been bullied for their more "nerdy" qualities. But he once had to intervene when one boy was bullied because he brought sugary snacks to school instead of the organic tofu snacks that his classmates brought in their recycled lunch boxes. Were these kids bullying the boy out of actual concern for his health, or were they merely acting out the more exclusive and tribal aspects of human behavior? Consider also the phenomenon of "moral licensing," on display when people tend to buy more junk food when shopping with reusable canvas bags[12] or when they purchase more beer or ice cream after picking up healthier options like kale.[13] We seem to think that our karma will balance out and we can then "spend" it on less-than-ideal behaviors. As always, it's a better option to follow the middle path. Nina Mažar, an associate professor of marketing at the University of Toronto, believes that the more we tie our identity and ego to virtue, the more likely we are to succumb to moral licensing. The best way to develop a habit of ethical behavior is to make it a habit without taking overt pride in it and without letting ego get heavily involved.[14]

The point is, being too strict with ourselves or our kids can backfire. Overly strict, "authoritarian" parenting styles come with their own problems, including children who are better liars![15] One high school senior I worked with had parents who were so controlling of her money that they demanded receipts for every purchase she made. When her mom found the girl taking a twenty out of her purse, there was no excuse, and yet the conditions were ripe for the girl to steal the money to assert her independence about her decisions. We need to allow some *give* with our children, because there will definitely be some *take*. We want to raise kids to recognize the principles behind rules rather than the exact letter of the law. Again, consider a guardrail on the highway. If the guardrail is too close to the road, we are more likely to scrape against it, and that doesn't really keep us safe either. Having ethical standards allows us to know when those standards are slipping. Our ethics can also teach us about ourselves, especially when we are under stress or when no one else is watching.

reflection What are some ways your ethical guardrails can teach you about your spiritual condition? What are your triggers and red flags for slipping into behaviors you aren't proud of?

Consistency as Ethical Behavior

We like our coworkers, friends, and politicians to be consistent, and we know that the best thing we can give our kids for stable emotional development is consistency. But doing so can prove challenging when we are constantly told by the media, in-laws, and other parents that we are doing the wrong thing and should try something new. Choosing the right brand of baby toothpaste is confusing enough, but it's nothing compared to the choices in sleep training, discipline, and feeding, all of which come free with the judgment of others! I am often astonished at the size and diversity of the bookstore's parenting section, and I'm baffled by how much conflicting advice it contains, as well as how rare it is to have this advice backed with actual science. In our culture of choice and diversity, it seems like each year offers a new bestseller extolling the virtues of so-called Asian parenting, French parenting, Danish parenting, Mexican parenting, and so on. And here I am offering this book on parenting with Eastern wisdom. If all of these works have great points to make, how do we choose among them?

When I started out as a therapist, I relied a lot on a trusted supervisor's thoughts on parenting styles. He had three kids and is a child development guy. For each of his children, he used a different method of sleep training, and even a different style of parenting. Turns out, each kid is fine, *because* each kid is different. But whatever parenting approach you pick, whichever therapist's advice you follow or book you read that resonates for you, stick it out for a while with your co-parent, checking in with each other and a trusted expert. The most confusing thing for kids is an inconsistent approach, where the parents switch up their style every few months with the latest fad. And it's not even just chasing fads—it's hard to be consistent, and once again you don't have to be perfect, just consistent *enough*.

Consistency is especially important when it comes to discipline.[16] Consequences should be clear and predictable. So kids can connect them to the event, they are ideally timely and reflect or include natural consequences that the "real world" would offer. If you do need to switch gears and try a new approach to discipline, stick with it and keep communicating with your partner. New behavior plans with kids almost inevitably make matters worse before they get better, so expect that. Any strong action leads to a strong reaction, whether it's in behavior or particle physics. Give yourselves a few weeks or a month to follow through with the change—not just a few days—and try to be as patient and compassionate with yourself and your co-parent. Your child's behavior has likely been conditioned over years, so it will take time to change.

Ethical Dilemmas

External guides such as precepts, commandments, and family rules are useful, but they only get us so far when things get sticky. When that happens, we need to turn to our teachers and our own inner wisdom for help. In the end, our ethics have to come from a balance of within and without, so that they are rule-guided rather than rule-governed. Ideally, this will carry over into the lives of our children and how they follow their own ethics.

In my work and home life, I'm not always sure what's the right thing to do. In those situations, I find it helpful to look at the issue from the other side—that is, I try to get clear on what the wrong approaches are. What happens when I choose to take the easy way out? What results from me spending too much time at work or on the Internet? What comes from me lashing out in anger? I also find that doing nothing is sometimes the right action, but I can't do nothing as a passive choice—it must be an active decision.

Even so, the best action is often unclear. In those cases, it's helpful for me to recall a story about the Buddha's relationship with his own son, Rāhula. The Buddha advised his son to reflect on the consequences of his actions three times—before, during, and after. He also told Rāhula to investigate whether the actions served all beings, including himself. So if I want to know if a particular behavior is ethical for me, I try this out, and then I meditate about it later to contemplate how I would feel if my own child acted that way. You can do this, too. Try sitting on your meditation cushion after you lie to your partner or snap at your kids. For me, doing so erodes my tendency toward smug self-satisfaction; often within a few minutes, I either want to quit meditating or make amends and restore harmony.

Most spiritual and philosophical traditions encourage self-reflection, particularly when our lives get messy or rough. Maybe we should rephrase our "Go to your room and think about what you've done!" to "Go to your room and think about what you are going to do, and think about it as you are doing it, and then after you do that, think about what you've done, and also think about how what you've done has affected others." That may not be entirely realistic, but the point is that reflection doesn't have to be heavy or guilt-ridden. It can even be fun to exercise our ethical muscles with hypothetical scenarios. Ethical debates can really get a family conversation going at the dinner table. Try these questions and see what happens:

- Is it right to steal if you can't afford food?

- Is it okay to break the speed limit if you are rushing to the hospital?

- How hard should you look for the owner of a lost toy? If you don't find the owner, is it okay to keep the toy?

- If a store clerk charges you too little for a purchase, should you mention it?

Discuss ethical conundrums that occur in real life, too. You'll surely encounter these in your child's social life, their English and history textbooks, current events, and even music.

Conclusion: Why Ethics Help Our Children Thrive

The wisdom and science behind ethics are simple: when we act skillfully, we feel good and whole, and we don't suffer from the nagging cognitive dissonance or fear of being caught doing something harmful. As the saying goes, "When I do good I feel good, when I do bad I feel bad, and that's my religion." Our children can learn this guiding principle for themselves, but in the meantime, they learn more from our actions than from our words.

We can all make ethical behavior a habit. By thinking, speaking, and acting skillfully today, we and our children will be more likely to think, speak, and act skillfully tomorrow—it's that simple. We can create conditions that make it less likely for us to commit unskillful actions and make it easy to act with kindness and respect. Spiritual teachings and the research on ethics suggest that moral guidelines are not about restricting us; they are actually about giving us a clearer path to freedom and happiness.

Of course, we can't expect our children to be as ethically sophisticated as adults are supposed to be. As humans, we develop morally as we age, and a number of different theories explain this process. Sigmund Freud asserted that the superego develops at around the age of five as a type of conscience to hold the primitive id in check.[17] More recently, we have come to understand that the prefrontal cortex—the so-called seat of our moral compass—doesn't finish developing until early adulthood. So be patient! Your kids *will* invariably act selfish, at least for a while!

Parenthood means finding the right balance between letting our children grow into who they naturally are and encouraging them to be a certain way. Change doesn't only happen through force. When it comes to parenting, force and shame are blunt instruments with short-term gains and long-term problems. Lasting change at the individual and societal level comes through *ahimsa*—nonviolence—as evidenced by the brave efforts of Gandhi, Martin Luther King Jr., and countless others. In their cases, nonviolence worked because it brought out the best in their adversaries and encouraged all parties to compromise from a place of wisdom, rather than fear. Likewise, we want to bring out the best in our families and encourage them to bring out the best in others as they mature and encounter the inevitable conflicts and confusions of life.

Reminders and Reflections

- We practice ethical behavior to keep everyone safe and protected.

- We cultivate ethics in our children by embodying those ethics ourselves and pointing out skillful behaviors when we see them.

- It is inevitable that our kids will experiment to find what ethics and values make sense to them. Our job is to help them do that safely.

- The five **THINK** guidelines about speaking are helpful to follow: Is it **t**rue or **h**elpful? Am **I** the one to say it? Is it **n**ecessary, **n**ow? And is it **k**ind?

- Which of the five **THINK** guidelines about speaking is the most challenging for you and your family to practice?

- When do you and your children tend to react aggressively in thoughts, words, and actions? When is it easiest to react with kindness and patience?

- Growing up, what values were you taught about sexuality?

- Consider the five precepts not as commandments but as aspirations to practice being your best self.

- Start teaching your kids at an early age about sex and consent in a positive way.

- If you do have a conflict with your family, model resolving it in healthy ways, showing that it's okay to disagree, while also demonstrating that everyone is safe.

- Encourage conversations and friendly debates with your children about ethics.

CHAPTER 3

less is more parenting

(Raising Renunciation—Nekkhamma)

Do everything with a mind that lets go. Don't accept praise
or gain or anything else. If you let go a little, you a will have
a little peace; if you let go a lot, you will have a lot of peace;
if you let go completely, you will have complete peace.

BUDDHIST PROVERB

My son's first sentence was "thank you," confirming our suspicions
that we were the parents of the century. His next phrase, however, was
"I want that," followed soon after with "I don't want that," usually ren-
dered in an earsplitting scream. We quickly realized that we'd created
a human being with desires and dislikes after all. Whether babies or
adults, we all want what we want when we want it. And in our current
culture, many of us *can* get the things we want when we want them. As
a result, we're swimming in stuff, but we are hardly any happier.

Despite smaller families, we now own bigger houses, we drive
bigger cars, and our kids have more toys than ever before. With the
rise in cheap labor, prices have dropped on almost everything, from
toys to clothes and more. We can get almost anything we desire
delivered to our doorstep with the click of a button, maybe even by
drone. Despite enormous houses, Americans now spend billions on
storage space. New technologies offer us instant access to entertainment anywhere we go, and changes in agriculture give us food that's

way cheaper and often less nutritious. Literally and figuratively, we are awash in empty calories.

All this "freedom of choice" in everything from toothpaste to parenting styles actually makes us more stressed and lonely, less happy, and even less motivated.[1] In October 1998, the satirical newspaper *The Onion* announced, "Consumer Product Diversity Now Exceeds Biodiversity," satirizing our culture's carelessness about the environment and our consumer culture, all in one joke. As our options as consumers grow in the Western world, our happiness dwindles. In fact, Western cultures lead the world in depression, anxiety, and mental illness at all ages.[2,3]

Monastics and clergy of different traditions take a vow of poverty, relinquishing the comforts of this life. I'm not suggesting that you toss all your possessions to find happiness for your family—even the Buddha found a middle path between renouncing his inherited riches and living the harsh life of a wandering ascetic. But new parents often do make sacrifices, just without the vow. Consider everything you've had to give up as a parent—comfort, sleep, space, time, money, career advancement, intimacy with your partner, and more. It doesn't take us very long as new parents to quickly abandon the dreams of white upholstery on the couch or spontaneous long weekends out of town. We often give up exercise and long leisurely meals. And mothers give up their body as something wholly their own. We forget all hopes of being cool—it's letting go not only of those weeknight rock concerts but also to the idea that we can remain remotely dignified as we change a diaper on a screaming child in public. We sacrifice physical and mental space and often our own mental health. Think about it: we have become preoccupied with one creature every single day for the rest of our lives. And yet, we do all of this for love.

The word *renunciation* may sound harsh. That's why I prefer the terms *simplification*, *letting go*, or even *making space*. When my wife was pregnant, we spent a lot of time worrying about what we'd lose, until my friend Harris pointed out that giving up my motorcycle or sacrificing vacations in Borneo weren't for nothing. "It's not like you don't gain something for what you give up," he reminded us. So we trade some familiar enjoyments for something more meaningful and deeper. We exchange the joy of "freedom" for the joy of connection, the joy of independence for interdependence.

reflection What are some ways your priorities have shifted since becoming a parent?

Types of Attachment

Traditional Buddhism describes four types of attachment that we will examine in this chapter. These essentially give us four types of letting go—attachments to pleasures and things, to unhealthy habits, to "wrong view" (limiting beliefs, emotional baggage, resentments, etc.), and to our sense of self and identity.

Letting Go of Stuff

Despite giving up so much when becoming parents, we ironically enter a whole new world of stuff—some necessary, but most not so much. With each child, the average household inventory expands another 30 percent.[4] In the United States, we have 3 percent of the world's children and 40 percent of the world's toys,[5] with the average child receiving 70 new toys a year—and that's according to research that's already a decade old.[6] And still we continue to buy more stuff, even when a majority of parents believe their own children are spoiled![7]

Some historians say that toys went from just being holiday gifts to becoming year-round purchases when the Mickey Mouse Club premiered in 1955.[8,9] Today, any thirty-minute TV show includes at least eight minutes of advertisements, and much of the television programming for kids is rarely more than a twenty-two-minute commercial for tie-in toys or other merchandise. Even when they turn off their screens, our children are barraged with advertisements for toys, games, and the latest gadgets—not to mention having such goodies placed at child height in grocery stores, pharmacies, coffee shops, and more. So if you think it's hard to resist, consider what you are up against. Corporations spend $17 billion a year marketing to kids—an almost 200-fold increase over the past thirty years.[10] Marketing firms hire the best behavioral scientists in the world, who use the latest technology, such as MRI machines, to better locate the "want" button in our brains.

Considering all we're up against, what can we do? For starters, we can explain to kids what marketing is and how it's designed to fool our brains. (Check out the Campaign for a Commercial-Free Childhood at commercialfreechildhood.org for some helpful ideas.) Next, we can set limits around buying toys and reserve gifts only for special occasions. This also gives kids something to look forward to (as opposed to expecting it), builds patience as they wait, enhances their appreciation, and makes them happier. Third, we can serve as healthy models by not overly engaging in retail therapy. If we regularly send the message to our kids that stuff buys happiness, we can't expect them to learn otherwise.

My parents' house—my teenage home—was recently destroyed in a fire. My parents are fine but lost nearly everything—books, clothing, heirlooms, and countless other possessions and comforts. I feel this loss, too, as the fire took not just my childhood memorabilia, but memories too. However, although this was heartbreaking and hard for all of us, there was also a strange relief, as if the loss of that house and its objects had lifted some kind of burden from us.

Deliberately (or accidentally, as in the case of the fire) getting rid of literal burdens is a liberating practice. As Bob Dylan said in "Like a Rolling Stone," "When you ain't got nothin', you got nothing to lose." In the recent bestseller *The Life-Changing Magic of Tidying Up*, Marie Kondo offers some simple advice for letting go of material things. For example, she suggests looking over each thing you own and asking yourself, "Does this spark joy?" If it does, keep it. If it doesn't, express your gratitude for the purpose that thing once served and wish it a fond farewell.[11] We can practice this with our children by regularly sorting through old toys and clothes, appreciating the items that still spark engagement and happiness, and enjoying the extra room we gain by saying goodbye to the things that don't.

Kids need "mastery" of their toys, not superficial relationships with as many possessions as possible. You probably noticed early on in your child's life that kids want the same books and games over and over again. The repetition might drive us adults crazy, but it's actually critical for a child's cognitive development. When kids have too many toys—even more than five at once—they are less able to focus enough to learn from and master them.[12] You've also likely witnessed how creative and engaged kids become when they have to invent new toys and games out of virtually nothing. If necessity is the mother of invention, perhaps boredom is its father.

Research clearly backs the benefits of fewer toys. One telling study from Germany explored removing toys from a nursery school for three months. While the first days were tough for kids and staff alike, by the end of three months, the kids were playing more creatively, communicating and cooperating more effectively, and concentrating far longer than in their previously toy-filled classroom.[13] Somehow, after a certain point, the more toys kids have, the more they seem to fight about them.

Yet, letting go is hard. Humans have been wired through evolution to believe that having more—more stuff, more food, more entertainment—will make us safer and happier, even when we have more than enough. For example, people are less likely to part with things they've spent "good money" on—a psychological principle known as the "sunk-cost fallacy" (though studies show that practicing mindfulness reduces this effect[14]). Yet most of us know that getting rid of things usually leads to more relief than regret.

With kids, consider engaging their imagination and natural compassion. For example, ask which toys are lonely or which stuffed animals might be happier (and might bring happiness) in a new home. Imagining the story of that toy's next journey can help make the thank-you and goodbye that much easier. As parents, we can have trouble letting go of our kids' tiny sweaters, first finger paintings, and miniature baby shoes, but when we purge most of the old stuff, we treasure what we keep that much more.

You could also set up a toy swap or a donation drive. Entrepreneurial kids can sell their old toys and spend the money on something new or donate that money to a good cause. A few years ago, I was jogging past a child's yard sale in my neighborhood. I asked what they were using the money for, and the smiling seven-year-old informed me, "It's for a charity that helps women trapped in abusive marriages." Sometimes the motivation for letting go can be as simple as helping others.

Some degree of simplification doesn't have to mean becoming an ascetic—monks and martyrs don't usually have families to provide for, after all. But keep in mind that less is more—more space, more time, more money, more creativity, more gratitude, and more harmony and happiness. And yet, despite the romantic fantasies we may have harbored of our kids blissfully playing only with handcrafted wooden toys and contemplating nature, we also want them to be able to experience enough toys and culture so that they can connect with other kids.

reflection How much stuff does your family actually need? Are there things that immediately come to mind that you could donate or sell? By getting rid of some of your stuff, what might you immediately gain?

Renouncing Unhealthy Habits

The second type of attachment and letting go has to do with unhelpful and unhealthy habits. Specifically, I want to talk about our Western addiction to busyness. Filling our time with activity is almost expected of us, and we certainly don't want others to see us as lazy. We are entertained when we are busy, and being busy also makes us feel important. But the habit of so much rushing becomes self-reinforcing to the point of absurdity.

Adults always seem to suffer from a lack of free time, but kids too are now missing out on free hours to play, explore, get curious, and just reflect. We shuttle our overscheduled children from school to sports and other after-school activities before bringing them home to a crushing mountain of homework. College-bound kids try to fill their résumés with an astonishing array of experiences and talents, leaving them exhausted jacks-of-all-trade and masters of none. Meanwhile, packed calendars leave kids with a sense of "learned helplessness;" they often feel as if they have little control over their own lives, stifling resilience, motivation, and determination, as well as setting the stage for depression and anxiety.

Sports have taken on greater and greater significance in the past decades, leading to overuse injuries in ever-younger children that were once seen only in professional athletes.[15] Not to mention the growing cost of equipment, league fees, specialized summer training clinics, and individual coaches, plus the hours of driving across the state to tournaments. But it's not just sports. One of my young patients informed me that he had to miss a session the following week because his team had made it to the statewide competition. "I didn't know you did a sport," I responded. "No, our drama team!" he explained. While it's wonderful to see the arts elevated in this way, we don't need to make everything a make-or-break competition. From mathletes to national robotics competitions to a cappella sing-offs, so many activities that our kids once just did for fun have become work to polish the college résumé instead of mere fun.

But what if we were to renounce at least some of this overstructured time and the professionalization of every activity and find a middle path—a healthy balance of structured and unstructured time to let kids freely play, explore, develop new insights, and make their own discoveries? Some leading companies have begun to implement a "20-percent time" program, in which employees can spend 20 percent of their time freely working on their own projects. At Google, this policy led to the creation of such products as Gmail and Google Maps. If this works so well for adults, perhaps we should consider a 20-percent time program at home and school.

Regardless of how we do it, it's important to push back in some way against the crazy homework culture, which doesn't remotely correlate with long-term learning. On top of that, we can deescalate the extracurriculars and advanced placement arms race and emphasize instead interest, passion, and follow-through, not to mention kindness. In good news, in a conversation I recently had with an Ivy League admissions officer, she explained that while elite colleges have long been able to identify and recruit top academic and athletic performers, they are now working on ways to identify those kids with deep passions, positive leadership attributes, and true community-mindedness at a young age and recruit them.

reflection   How overscheduled are your children? How much actual joy and discovery are they getting out of their extracurricular activities? How much of your family time is taken up with shuttling your child from place to place?

For adults and children alike, the way most of us keep ourselves busy these days is through technology. Ideally, technology makes our lives easier and more connected, but we often use it in ways that stress us out and disconnect us more. A recent statistic showed that children *and* adults average nine hours of screen time daily, checking our devices about 150 times a day, almost none of which we are doing with full intention and attention.[16] Mindlessly surfing the Internet or checking our social media is actually making us all unhappier. But remember, the power is in your hands—if the news makes you unhappy, don't check it so often. If social media leads to too many unhappy comparisons, "hide" those parents with the smugly perfect family vacation photos. And remember, you don't have to answer yes to every friend request.

Our screens are addictive to all of us, but they are especially addictive for children. And yet, we can't expect our children to navigate their lives without screens—like it or not, screens are here to stay. Our kids rely on them for their homework, news, and social lives. But we can help them better manage how and when they use their devices, especially at home. When play is too screen-focused, kids' brains fail to wire for social understanding, empathy, and emotional intelligence. The more kids play online, not looking at each other; it's no surprise that so many kids grow up struggling to read facial expressions and body language. Eye contact with other humans is crucial for securing early attachment and emotional regulation. With kids interacting mainly with smooth, flat surfaces, it's no wonder they struggle with sensory integration. Children play reactive video games that do little to help them learn to delay gratification or develop patience or impulse control. Even technologies designed and intended for educational purposes can hinder growth—those Baby Einstein videos and talking toys may actually curb language and cognitive development at a young age.[17]

New brains overstimulated with technology paired with under-stimulated young bodies make an unhealthy combination that hinders brain integration and healthy bodies. Fortunately, pediatricians have recently set some fairly clear guidelines for screen time: nothing for infants (except for video chats), an hour max for ages two to five, and no more than two hours from five on. When our kids do begin to interact with screens, we can talk through what they are seeing, just as we would with a book. More than anything, kids need genuine interpersonal exchange, especially with parents who can show them lovingkindness and patience.

Screens may dominate waiting rooms, airplane lounges, and restaurants, but even if we have them at home, they don't have to dominate our lives. We can also make them less appealing. My own parents kept a lousy old black-and-white TV (without cable!) in an uncomfortable and out-of-the-way corner of the house, but they had books all throughout our home, which incentivized reading or going outside. My parents occasionally bought us toys for holidays, but they were far more generous with educational experiences and books. I was even allowed to extend my bedtime if I was reading.

If you can't diminish the dominance of screens at home, you can stress the importance of taking breaks from screens and everything else. Consider how many religions make a point of celebrating space and rest through Sabbaths, holidays, retreats, and other periods of downtime. This tradition has largely slipped out of our secular lives. But by making sacred time—or at least renouncing a certain kind of busyness from work or screens—we actually make more space in our lives to appreciate what matters, get much-needed rest, and reduce family stress. My wife and I try (with mixed success) to enjoy one

Sabbath day a week—no writing, no work emails, no business calls. We've found that doing so helps us relax and reconnect. What's more, mindfully creating space like this somehow makes more room to get things done the rest of the week. We procrastinate a lot less on Friday when we know that Saturday will be family day. Sabbaths don't have to be entire days, of course. You can start by spending a moment in silence or gratitude before family dinners, and you can mark the preciousness of those meals by staying off of your devices. Whatever you choose to try, don't do it halfway. When you have to work, excuse yourself and work—don't feel guilty; it's okay if you have to work. But when you are with your kids, be fully present, not partially eyeing your phone or laptop.

Another option is to renounce screens by place—no devices at the dinner table or in certain rooms, or only on long car trips (not just while driving around town). One friend requests that her family leave their phones by the door when they come home, and many parents require that their kids charge their phones overnight in the kitchen. Another friend leaves his phone in the car while he shops. Merely having our phones in view cuts down on conversation, so it's a good idea to put your phone out of sight during family time.

Of course, most schools require technology so kids can be technologically fluent, and yet I can't think of a time I heard of a kid who needed special accommodations because they couldn't figure out an iPad. There is something to the argument that we need to give kids screens so they can learn to manage them. But just think about it: we don't hand over crack and suggest kids learn how to manage it. Rather it's our job to show and teach them how to manage a reasonable amount of screen time; and keep them away from crack.

reflection   What aspects of your relationship with technology would you like to change? How can you make more time and space for your family? As a child, what were the special times when you felt closest as a family?

Discarding Harmful Views

We inherit a lot from our families—wonderful family heirlooms, meaningful traditions, and some healthy values. But we also inherit some old things we don't want—not just those inexplicable knickknacks, but also the inexplicable memories, habits, and beliefs that we'd rather not pass on to our own kids. Ideally, we take the best of what our own family and culture bequeathed us and let go of the unhelpful aspects of our inheritance. In fact, as parents, this becomes our responsibility. *We* have to do the work of exorcising the ghosts of our ancestors, the trauma of our grandparents, and the addictions of our in-laws, because no one else will. No one else can.

Whether we call it the "repetition compulsion," epigenetics, or karma, we are not doomed to repeat the mistakes and troubles of our ancestors. But not doing so takes work. The work begins with an understanding that we can let go of the belief that we are fated to repeat the past. While my friend Jack anxiously awaited his son's birth, he was simultaneously caring for his aging, alcoholic father. Despairing the disconnected relationship with his dad, he tearfully confessed to his therapist, "I just don't want my son to dread dealing with me someday, to dread my calls or visits. And it breaks my heart to know that day will eventually come." His therapist just smiled and reminded him, "Jack, it doesn't *have* to be that way." So, first of all, we can examine, question, and let go of our limiting beliefs about the future.

We can also say goodbye to the belief that we aren't good enough parents, though that thought will probably return again and again. What if we could let go of all the guilt by renouncing the word *should* from our inner dialogue? How much more energy would we have? Try making a practice of noticing how often you say *should* over the next week.

What if we could also let go of limiting beliefs about who our children *should* be? Our culture wants so much to put our kids in categories—gifted or special needs, sick or healthy, mentally ill or recovering, above or below average on one measure or another. Yet most of us know that when we categorize people like this, it limits who they are and who they can become. In one famous study, teachers were told that random kids in their classes were gifted, and those particular children (who were actually "normal") excelled.[18] Imagine how this plays out when we look at children with actual learning differences or the biases that follow lower-income kids, children of color, or girls. Is it any surprise that we see chasms of achievement open up between different children? As we think and act, our world becomes. When children see themselves as being bad at a particular subject in school (whether or not they need help), failure becomes a self-fulfilling prophecy. Sometimes our kids will need support that can be gained through labels, but labeling them might also limit their possibilities.

We can also let go of our ideas of who we want our child to be, or we can at least try to do so. For no reason at all, my wife and I assumed that our first child would be a girl. When the ultrasound technician announced we'd be having a boy, my wife and I watched a whole story in our minds crumble away. My own therapist joked, "This is a good lesson for you two—he's not even born yet, and he's already let you down!" We all want great things for our children, but if we hold too tightly to our fantasies for their futures (their careers as doctors, their blissful relationships, their abundant offspring), we don't allow them the room to grow their own abundant, rich, and unique lives.

Letting Go of Identification

What's more, we can relinquish some of our culture's limiting beliefs about what a family is supposed to look like. This might mean letting go of gender roles or family structures that we imagined growing up, especially as our culture evolves. It might also mean questioning the assumptions of our community or larger family system about what constitutes a *good* parent. How much time are you supposed to take off from work before you qualify as a "good" parent? What type of diaper are you required to buy in order to be a "good" mother? What style of discipline makes you a "good" father?

By letting go of unhelpful and unhealthy ideas, we practice the wisdom of forgiveness. Whether we let go of the notion that we're bad parents, or that other people are irredeemably messed up, or that our partners are the root of all our problems, we can experiment with letting go as an act of kindness and generosity. As the adage says, "Forgiveness means giving up all hope for a better past." And there's plenty of research to back this up. Practicing forgiveness leads to increased emotional and psychological health, cultivates empathy, and even improves heart disease.[19] On the other hand, clinging to our resentments builds stress hormones like cortisol and adrenaline, affecting our ability to think creatively, promoting sickness and negativity, and suppressing our tendency toward compassion and empathy.[20] Hanging on to that anger will make you both sick and miserable.

PRACTICE Letting Go Visualization

Find a comfortable posture and relax as you take a few mindful breaths. After a few moments of relaxation, reflect on any resentments or other unhelpful beliefs you carry around with you on a daily basis. Choose a smaller belief that feels like something you could set aside for the rest of the day. What would it look like to not have to carry this resentment around with you?

Continue to breathe and relax as you visualize letting go of this workable belief. Release it from your grasp, just for now. If you have trouble letting go, remember that you can always pick up the belief again tomorrow.

After a few moments, take a few more deep breaths as you review the stories you tell yourself about your parenting. When was the last time you accused yourself of being a bad parent? How often have you leveled the accusation against yourself that you're just like your mother or father? Think about what it would be like to let these thoughts go. Imagine what it would feel like if you didn't require yourself to be perfect. What if you could live each day as a "good enough" parent?

Letting go is no easy feat. Remember: aim for the middle path. That means starting by becoming aware of what you really do and don't need in your life, whether it's stuff, habits, or beliefs. I once heard a meditation teacher say, "Being a monk is knowing you need to let go, but not being able to 90 percent of the time." Does this sound familiar, parent friends? Meanwhile, another friend of mine recently proclaimed that parenting is just one lifelong process of letting go. And when the letting go gets tough, recall the other Buddhist advice: "You don't have to let go; you just have to not hold on."

Reminders and Reflections

- When it comes to toys and activities, less is more for your child's cognitive, creative, and compassion development.

- Having too many choices is actually correlated with an increase in anxiety and unhappiness.

- Which type of letting go discussed in this chapter might bring you the biggest challenges?

- What expectations do you have for your children's future? Which ones are you willing to let go?

- Could you let go of, or not hold on to, your idea of what a perfect parent is supposed to look like?

- Use vacations and camping trips as opportunities to discuss how little you actually need and to practice sharing both space and stuff.

- Consider providing toys that leave room for creative imaginary play, not just single-purpose toys.

- If it's hard to let go of all your kids' toys, consider rotating some in and out of storage or rotating and trading with friends.

- Create and honor family time—be it dinners or days.

- Consider ways to create screen-free times and places.

CHAPTER 4

building a wiser brain

(Raising Wisdom—Panna)

When I was a boy of fourteen, my father was so ignorant
I could hardly stand to have the old man around.
But when I got to be twenty-one, I was astonished at
how much the old man had learned in seven years.

OFTEN ATTRIBUTED TO MARK TWAIN

While most of us know wisdom when we see it, how would you define wisdom when it comes to parenting, or how it pertains to a family or even your child? One definition of wisdom that has stuck with me is seeing things as they are and acting accordingly. Wisdom is that union of experience and knowledge that leads to insight, clarity, and skillful action. And yet wisdom in action is a moving target—the best thing to do today might not hold true tomorrow, and a wise action for your family might not be the best thing for mine.

Traditional Buddhism refers to three different types of wisdom: conceptual, experiential, and applied. As parents, you can find the first type of wisdom from reading up on child development or from books like this. You get the second type from the trial-and-error of your own life. The third type is what I hope you'll do by practicing the techniques offered here. Applied wisdom also means encouraging our kids to learn on their own through teachable moments, which will stick more than just telling them what to do.

Some of us are familiar with the functions of the different hemispheres of the brain (i.e., the left is language-centered, logical, and organized; the right controls creativity, experiences emotion, and intuits nonverbally). Neuroscientist Dan Siegel and parenting expert Tina Bryson go one step further; in their book, *The Whole-Brain Child*, they creatively describe "downstairs" and "upstairs" aspects of the brain.[1] Our primitive brains—the limbic system and amygdala—are reactive and emotional, driven by impulsive, short-term interests, and primitive drives. This childlike, impulsive, instinctual system lives downstairs. Meanwhile, the outer cortices of our brains, which enable us to inhibit impulses, slow down, gain perspective, process emotional stimuli, and articulate these stimuli into thought and action, live upstairs. This upstairs area helps us plan, think before we act, take perspective, make moral decisions, and form relationships.

According to Marsha Linehan, the creator of dialectical behavior therapy, the "wise mind" integrates both our emotional and our rational minds.[2] The four aspects of our brains—left, right, upstairs, downstairs—need strong connections of hallways and staircases, and we're at our best when they are connected and work together.

Building a Wise Mind and an Integrated Brain

Dan and Tina explain that in our kids, the outer cortices hang out "upstairs" in a somewhat messy construction site until early adulthood.[3] Because they are "under construction," young brains are highly plastic, meaning that their neural connections can change and develop easily, depending on experiences and how they are used. Just as we can influence the development of our children's physical bodies and muscles within certain parameters, we can actually help our children build and integrate their brains in healthy ways to become what they call a "whole-brain child." That means we can foster healthy development in the very structures of their brains, wiring them for insight, wisdom, and the other good stuff in this book.

Dan and Tina recommend integrating strong right-brain emotional experiences (frustration, fear, love, etc.) with their more logical, language-based left brains. For example, as parents, you can help your child "name and tame," as labeling strong emotions and creating a logical story engages the left brain to calm the right. This is the concept behind teaching kids to "use their words," even from a young age. You can also help children practice integration through art, dance, and music—anything to build a hallway between their left and right hemispheres that makes sense of their strong emotional experiences and helps them move on a little bit wiser. It is when kids can't or don't integrate strong emotions that they get stuck. Minor fears become phobias, a passing sadness can turn into a depressive episode, and mere frustration can explode into an anger problem. But with healthy guidance, kids gradually learn how to integrate their experiences on their own.

Of course, in the heat of the moment, this is easier said than done. Kids aren't able to receive or understand our coaching when activated emotionally. So, the experts recommend connecting first nonverbally. We attune our right brain to theirs by kneeling down to their height, offering an empathic sigh or sound, mirroring their body language and facial expressions, or offering a gentle hand on the back or hug if they are up for it (if not from us, then maybe from a beloved pet or stuffed animal). These direct "attend and befriend" responses actually connect us at the biological level, which means our kids can then feel safe enough to calm down and process more fully with their left brains.

Going deeper into Siegel and Bryson's "upstairs" and "downstairs" analogy again, we're trying to build a staircase between the reactive limbic system downstairs and the prefrontal cortex (PFC) upstairs. The PFC is associated with planning and thinking and is located just behind the forehead. It was the last part of the brain to evolve in humans, and it's the last to develop as we grow up, only reaching maturity in our mid-twenties (and, no surprise, even later in young men). In many ways, the PFC is what makes us human—it's where we contemplate the future, weigh options, control impulses, and regulate behavior. By inviting kids to help us plan shopping lists, choose weekend activities, and chime in on household decisions, we work out their PFCs and help them build their brains.

This isn't to say that the left and upstairs parts of the brain are better or wiser; it all depends on the situation at hand. When our child steps in front of traffic, mindfully labeling our emotions and then planning out the best angle at which to grab them isn't a priority—we just want to grab them and pull them to safety as fast as possible. The so-called lower brain enables us to do just that, partially by shutting off blood flow to the rest of the brain so we don't overthink the emergency. But we also don't want our kids to react to everything from fly balls to upcoming tests as if they were a life-threatening danger, just as we don't want them to respond to things like relationships or imminent dangers with a slow and calculating logic. Rather, we want our kids to operate with a balance of intention and intuition, developed by working out and integrating the various parts of their brains—left, right, upstairs, and down, inner and outer cortices that cultivate that "whole brain child."

Returning to Wise Mind

When the amygdala and emotions flare up, it's almost impossible for logic to penetrate our kids' closed-off outer cortices. Helping them settle down from a tantrum to engage their wise mind takes wisdom, compassion, and plenty of patience on our part. Our children are not miniature adults—their growing brains are actually incapable of taking an adult perspective on a situation and using that knowledge to calm down. Remembering this can help us see that tantrums are not methodically manufactured manipulations. A child's tantrum operates at an instinctual level that simply won't respond to reason. Once we recognize this, we can make more effective choices about responding. Yes, sometimes challenging behaviors are prefrontally premeditated, and in those cases, we should respond with intention, logic, and clear boundaries or consequences. However, when our kids are experiencing a limbic system meltdown, what they need is connection and calming.

When children descend into lower-brain chaos, we parents need to work overtime to first calm our own PFCs so we can view the situation clearly. When we show that we've regulated our own emotions, it signals to kids that it's safe for them to calm down. When we behave in this way, it also models and mirrors to them (often literally, through what are called mirror neurons) how to calm down. Thus, the quickest way to cultivate calm in a child is to practice being calm yourself. As one meme I recently saw on Twitter says, "Never in the history of calming down has anyone ever calmed down by being told to calm down." Telling kids to relax doesn't work nearly as well as a soft voice or a gentle touch, both of which turn on the "attend and befriend" response, shut off fight or flight, thin out cortisol, and boost oxytocin, the so-called love hormone. Once we establish that fundamental connection with our child (or anyone, for that matter), we can open our hearts and minds to each other, see each other's perspective, and move on together. Some child therapists even have kids "activate the symptom" or play-act at getting angry, only to then practice calming down with breathing, self-talk, or connecting exercises.

Once your child calms down and gets the PFC working again, you can move toward processing and planning verbally. You can even continue to engage the PFC by asking what consequence they think would be fair or asking them to reflect on why certain expectations exist in your household.

And don't forget your kids' basic needs. That PFC is an energy guzzler—sometimes just a rest or snack is all that's needed to get things up and running again. Of course, sometimes you have to get creative and throw your kid a curveball, maybe literally. In other words, you have to hijack their lower brain by getting them to do something with their bodies—playing catch or doing a few downward dogs. You can also engage their senses with strong sensory stimuli, like eating a bit of spicy food, smelling or tasting a lemon, or moving to a different room or getting outside. You can also try to jump-start their PFC with a seemingly random question, like what they want for dinner or what's the name of their best friend's mom. You can also decrease the dominance of the amygdala with games—a quick round of cards, some fun verbal wordplay, or a checkers match. From there, you can steer your kids back into their wisest minds.

When we interrupt tantrums like this, it's vital that, once things calm down, we address what triggered the tantrum. You don't have to rehash the details of every conflict. But remember that consistency is always key to raising resilient and healthy kids. So if you say you are going to come back to something later, come back to it. This lets kids integrate the experience with their whole brain once it's fully back online.

reflection   What are some successful techniques you already use to help your children calm themselves in moments of high emotion?

Use Your Words

When we can recognize and name an emotional experience, our brains become less reactive, and the energy flows back to the analytical parts of our brain, an effect on display in fMRI studies.[4] Especially when our children are younger, they may struggle to name their emotions. We can help them by using names for their feelings until they can internalize the skill (for example, "It seems like you are feeling anger toward your mom right now"), which is often similar to what I do and say as a therapist. This simple action immediately quiets the emotional limbic system, allowing kids to make sense of the experience and heal.

It also helps to talk about emotions in ways that keep us from overidentifying with those emotions. We can gently remind our kids that often when we feel sad, we believe we will always feel sad, and yet we need to remember that strong feelings don't last forever. Having even a little separation from our feelings helps pull us from "emotion mind" and back into wise mind. Saying "I feel sad" or "I'm having the thought that I'm sad," instead of "I am sad," identifies sadness as a state that will change, rather than an unchangeable trait. When we shift our mindset like this (more on this in chapter 8), we boost our ability to bounce back and recognize emotions as impermanent.

In my effort to console my son, I often catch myself saying things like, "You're okay!" when he definitely doesn't feel okay. This can be both confusing and invalidating. A better choice would be, "I know you feel sad right now—let's talk about why you feel that way." We can engage our kids in this way no matter what they're feeling in the moment (angry, fearful, or happy). We can even do this about feelings they had yesterday or feelings they might have tomorrow. Talking when kids are somewhat removed from the emotion helps them keep perspective when big feelings take over.

It's also important to remember that our kids *need* to feel bad from time to time, something that is often hard for us parents to tolerate. Negative feelings provide valuable information that helps us develop wisdom and make wise decisions in the future. Physically, pain can mean that something is wrong, but it can also mean we are pushing our physical limits in a healthy way that makes us stronger. With practice, we can learn to recognize which is which. The same is true emotionally. Strong feelings tell us a lot about ourselves and help us develop appropriate boundaries to stay safe. This particularly holds true for intuition, which gets a bad rap in some circles. I once had a supervisor tell me, "Obi-Wan was wrong: Don't trust your feelings. Feelings aren't facts." But feelings actually do offer a lot of useful information, especially when examined in the wise light of mindfulness.

Young children experience the world concretely in black-and-white terms, but as they get older, we want them to develop a more nuanced understanding of their emotional experience and the world. To foster this, we can practice using a range of words to describe emotions. With young kids, it's a good idea to start with a small set of options ("mad," "glad," or "sad"). We can then add to the color palette of the human emotional experience as they age. Paul Ekman, the psychologist and researcher who consulted on the recent Pixar hit *Inside Out*, describes the five basic human emotions: anger, sadness, joy, disgust, and fear. Todd VanDerWerff and Christophe Haubursin organized these into a useful chart that demonstrates the ways emotions overlap.[5]

	Joy	Sadness	Disgust	Fear	Anger
Joy	Ecstasy	Melancholy	Curiosity	Surprise	Righteousness
Sadness	Melancholy	Despair	Self-Hatred	Anxiety	Betrayal
Disgust	Curiosity	Self-Hatred	Prejudice	Revulsion	Loathing
Fear	Surprise	Anxiety	Revulsion	Terror	Hatred
Anger	Righteousness	Betrayal	Loathing	Hatred	Rage

Funny faces feelings–check-in charts and colorful mood meters have also been shown to be helpful for kids and are fun for the family. Having a broader palette of emotional colors to choose from cultivates a greater emotional quotient (EQ), a quality more important in relationships and job success than IQ alone.[6] As I once heard at a conference, "IQ gets you the job; EQ helps you rise to the top." We can help our kids develop their EQ by encouraging them to explore the range of emotions they feel, as well as the spectrum of feelings of others (friends, pets, or characters on TV or in books). We can also invite them to inspect the layers of complex feelings—for example, the sadness beneath the anger or the fear beneath the pain. Doing so will water the seeds of their innate empathy and kindness.

reflection   What are some creative ways you can help your family explore their emotions and discuss them in more nuanced ways to develop more wisdom?

Clear Seeing through Gratitude

According to my friend and mentor Christopher Germer, gratitude and appreciation are wisdom practices because they allow us to see more clearly. As humans, we evolved with a negativity bias—we had to focus more on the negative and potentially dangerous aspects of our environment in order to survive. An adage from positive psychology notes that our brains act like Velcro for the negative and Teflon for the positive. Unfortunately, the genetic wiring that kept our ancestors safe thousands (millions, really) of years ago often gets in the way of flourishing emotionally in today's world. To see clearly, we need to correct our negativity bias, and we do that by deliberately acknowledging what's good, right, and positive in our lives.

This might sound a little idealistic. However, practicing gratitude and appreciation most certainly does not mean going around pretending as if there were only positive things happening in the world, all the while denying the suffering and pain that we and others experience. Nothing could be further from the truth. Gratitude simply allows us to see it all, while recognizing that it takes extra effort to note and appreciate the positive. A patient of mine said it best: "Oh, I get it—it's not that I'm pretending the dog shit isn't there, it's that I'm also noticing the sunshine." It's important to acknowledge when there's dog shit in our lives (for obvious reasons), but it's equally important to enjoy the sunshine.

When we fail to notice the positive, we merely add to our stress levels, which tends to kick our negativity bias into high gear, which makes us more anxious and unhappy, and so on. We tend to overlook the good the more stressed we are, because our brains are scanning for danger—but the good is still there, and we need to tune into it. This reminds me of when my son was almost one and I suddenly noticed playgrounds all over the place. They had always been there; I just hadn't been looking for them. Appreciation is also like this—it attunes us to the positive, just like being a parent attunes us to things like playgrounds. And when we practice formally for long enough, we go from consciously and deliberately noticing the good to unconsciously noticing it. Thich Nhat Hanh offers an appreciation practice called the "non-toothache." It feels terrible to have a toothache, but once it goes away, we usually forget how bad the pain felt. So we can enjoy the relief and ease of the "non-toothache" we're experiencing in the moment.

We can promote the practice of appreciation with our families in a number of ways—noticing the beautiful trees on the way to school, savoring a meal with all of our senses, or relaxing into our favorite music. We can recall happy memories and successes, and we can plan events to look forward to. All of this boosts our mood not just in the moment; it also gives us happiness, wisdom, and perspective in longer-lasting ways.

PRACTICE Tuning in the Positive

Jot down three to five things that are going well right now in your life or things for which you feel grateful. These can be about yourself, your family, or any other aspects of your life, and they don't need to be huge. When you're done, read your list out loud and really take time to bring each thing to mind, noticing any shifts you might feel in your emotional experience and any sensations that come up in your body. It takes a mere instant to encode a negative experience into our internal "evidence file," while it takes up to thirty seconds for positive events to really set in. So, when something good comes to mind, contemplate it in mind and body for half a minute or so, and allow that positive experience to make a lasting impact on the makeup of your nervous system. You can help your kids do this, too, by having them go into detail when relaying something that made them happy or proud. Taking time to draw or write about a positive experience also allows the time for it to really sink in.

I encourage you to try this practice for yourself, if only for a week or two, to see if it subtly changes your perception of events. You will likely find that gratitude actually *feels* good. Maybe this explains why Americans overwhelmingly rank Thanksgiving as our favorite holiday.

Other holidays can be perfect times for appreciation, too. At some point, my wife and I created a New Year's Eve tradition of reflecting with gratitude on the previous year. We now send thank-you letters to everyone who helped us out along the way (sure beats the eye-roll-inducing holiday letter bursting with family accomplishments). Some friends keep a family gratitude jar throughout the year—as good things come up, family members drop small notes about those experiences in the jar. Then they all sit together to read those notes on New Year's day or birthdays.

Of course, we don't have to wait until the end of the year—or even the end of the day—to practice gratitude. At any point in the day, we can write a letter of thanks to an old friend or send a brief text. We can tell our spouse or child something we truly appreciate about them. And, of course, we can do this in ways that feel natural and fun. A friend and I actually tried to market an appreciation game called "Grategories" that involved alphabet dice and various categories of gratitude. We can also just make simple lists. Since I began making gratitude lists, I started to notice that I was looking for positive things to put on my list. In other words, I have unconsciously created a confirmation bias toward the fact that things are pretty good. You don't need to make the list every day—three or four times a week might be best. That way, you won't feel bad when you forget, end up repeating too much, or feel like you are forcing it.

Like practicing anything, from exercise to meditation, gratitude is easier to practice with others. Some friends and I started a gratitude group on Facebook that inspires each of us to make our lists. This group has kept a dozen of us connected around positivity for years now. You can build family connections around positive connections, especially with teens who often bond through negativity (making fun of annoying teachers, complaining about food, labeling certain music as "lame"). In short, don't keep gratitude to yourself—share your appreciation with each other.

reflection What are some ways you could cultivate gratitude on a regular basis? How can you make gratitude a habit or ritual in your family?

Practicing gratitude helps us see the world more clearly, but it also results in increased happiness, improved health, better grades, more connection, and elevated compassion and generosity, not to mention less materialism and envy.[7] Gratitude and appreciation give us perspective on other people's situations and enable us to maintain hope even in the face of tragedy. As Fred Rogers famously noted, even when disaster strikes, there will always be people doing their best to help others. "When I was a boy," he recalled, "I would sometimes see scary things in the news. My mother would comfort me by saying, 'Look for the helpers. You will always find people who are helping.' And I came to see that the world is full of doctors and nurses, police and firemen, volunteers, neighbors, and friends who are ready to jump in to help when things go wrong."[8]

Making Time to Connect and Reflect

Reflecting on the day at bedtime is a great way to connect with your children. This ritual helps them integrate their emotional experience into hard-earned wisdom. With so much busyness in our lives, we lose time to reflect. Offering your children a recurring ritual to do so gives them opportunities to talk out challenges or conflicts in their lives, including those they might have with you. Even when your kid is more reluctant to talk, the ritual can still help make a habit of reflecting at the end of each day.

Although focusing on the positive is important, we certainly need to tolerate and learn from the hard things in life, too. A popular practice among family therapists is the "roses and thorns" reflection—at dinnertime, each family member names one positive thing (rose) and one challenge (thorn) that occurred during the day. Although your kids will inevitably hit the age when they respond with eye rolls, they'll at least have the opportunity to ask *themselves*, thereby internalizing the reflection process.

There are lots of other ways to encourage reflection and agency in your kids. When something goes well in their lives, ask specifics about what they did. When things go poorly, invite them to problem-solve with you. As your kids share what's happening in their lives, consider engaging them with the following questions:

- What did you learn?

- Who helped you?

- What surprised you?

- How could things have gone differently?

- What would you do differently next time?

Without weighing your kids down by sharing every personal challenge you face, you can find ways to model this reflection practice by talking about your own experiences:

- What went well for you during the past week?

- Who do you want to thank?

- How could you avoid a particular problem in the future?

- What makes it difficult to recognize the good?

- What accomplishments are you most proud of?

We don't just have to *review* the past; we can also *preview* the future by planning ahead with our family. This can help your kids more accurately anticipate challenges and brainstorm strategies for getting through them, instead of blowing fears out of proportion and fixating on all the bad things that could happen. When we actively review our days and anticipate the future, even the unpleasant parts, we can put them into perspective by considering the context. We can then play the whole movie in our heads, including the boring stuff. For example, "If I looked at the list after school and didn't get picked for the team, I'd be really sad. Then I'd talk to my friends about it and probably cry for a while. Then I'd still get on the bus and go home, I'd have a snack with Nana, and then play outside with my brother, and then have dinner and do homework." Studies find that when we think through every other boring thing in the day in addition to the setback, we more accurately predict our responses and feelings and handle the adversity with newfound resiliency.[9] As an added bonus, thinking through future scenarios leads to more ethical choices and boosts our planning and executive functions.

Our Bodies: Where We Might Find Our Wise Mind

Our bodies are often the first places we experience emotions; they hold a tremendous amount of wisdom. Top athletes, performers, and those in other high-stress professions tend to have greater body awareness and *interoception*—the ability to listen to their body's inner signals and to self-regulate accordingly.[10] With practice, you can learn to tune in to your gut feelings and what your heart knows by literally turning your attention to these parts of the body. We have so many nerve endings around the heart and gut, and they give us the deep emotional wisdom we need for challenging decisions. After all, nature has wired us to be parents, and listening deeply to ourselves and our own nature is more likely to reveal an answer than any advice book.

Wisdom may not be the first quality we typically associate with kids and adolescents, but we can water the seeds of wisdom even in young children. Through experience, encouragement, and guidance, they (and we) can learn to trust intuition, gain wisdom from mistakes, and respond (rather than react) to life's challenges.

Reminders and Reflections

- Some aspects of our brains (the limbic system and amygdala) are reactive and emotional, and others (the higher and outer cortices) enable us to act with intention and wisdom. We need all of them working together to build wise, healthy brains.

- Young brains are "under construction" and can be trained to act with insight and wisdom.

- As parents, regulating our own emotions is the most effective way to help our kids regulate theirs.

- What are some examples of wisdom in your daily life that you can point out to your children?

- How can you encourage your family to articulate their emotions in nuanced ways?

- In nighttime reflections, consider the virtues in this book: What was a moment when your kids used patience or wisdom? Did they witness any acts of determination or kindness?

- Practice gratitude together as a family, either formally or informally.

- Take time daily to connect and reflect on the day's events with your child.

- Tune in to the wisdom of your own body, especially when you face a thorny problem.

CHAPTER 5

even the buddha had helicopter parents

(Raising Energy—Viriya)

Where would I find enough leather
To cover the entire surface of the earth?
But with leather soles beneath my feet,
It's as if the whole world has been covered.

SHANTIDEVA

Too many of us exhaust ourselves trying to create a perfectly safe world for our children. Instead, we can more wisely use our energy to teach our family to be safe in a world that is often frightening and dangerous. You've heard the descriptions and maybe even leveled them at others or yourself: *helicopter parents* (hovering above and behind), *snowplow parents* (clearing the path to adulthood), *bubble-wrapped teens*, and more. Yet, despite increased parental involvement and best intentions, our children have somehow wound up more fragile and less prepared for a world that is even safer than in generations past. Although we expend a lot of effort, we're not embodying the kind of wise use of our energy that the Buddhist monk Shantideva suggests in the opening quote.

In many ways, we have actually created a world that is safer than ever: we've coated our once-perilous playgrounds with rubber; bike

helmets, seatbelts, and airbags have become the norm; allergy awareness has kept kids safer; and academic accommodations for different
learning styles and abilities have succeeded in helping more kids learn
more effectively. Yet, parents and children express more anxiety than
ever before, and allowing a kid to walk alone to the playground is
enough to warrant a visit from the police.

But covering the world in a protective layer of rubber (or leather) has
backfired. A recent article in the *New York Times* exposed how an over-
emphasis on safety in modern playgrounds has resulted in kids being
less able to discern healthy risks from true dangers, leaving them more
vulnerable in the long run.[1] Many of us enjoyed the thrills of seesaws,
towering metal slides, and rickety hand-hammered tree houses. But how
many of these do you see today? Research psychologists now believe that
kids need to regularly face moderate dangers, take healthy risks, and
master those dubious structures—earning stitches and skinned knees in
the process—in order to meet and assess real-world challenges and risks
as they arise. In the past, we worried that kids who fell from the jungle
gym and broke their arm would invariably become afraid of heights
(and their city afraid of lawsuits). In reality, we now know that a child
who suffers a significant fall before turning nine is *less* likely to develop a
fear of heights.[2] Children require exposure to developmentally appropriate fears and setbacks in order to work through them and grow stronger.

A famous maxim tells us that "character cannot be developed in
ease and quiet." Most of us intuitively know this to be true—our kids
need *some* stress so they can build their own strength and directly learn
from overcoming challenges. It doesn't matter how involved we are in
our kids' lives—no degree of protection will keep them perfectly safe
from skinned knees and stubbed toes at age seven, or broken hearts
and B minuses in adolescence, or rowdy roommates and rejected
résumés by adulthood. I've worked with parents who schedule their
teenager's life down to fifteen-minute increments or constantly keep
track of their college student's movements by GPS. Although I believe
they have their children's best interests at heart, they've clearly over-
done it. While they may be the extremes, let's face it—we've all had
our moments.

Where do these efforts get us? What is the result of this type of overprotective energy? Studies indicate that so-called helicopter parenting styles might keep kids physically and emotionally safe, but they also correlate with higher rates of depression and anxiety, difficulties with executive function, and lower rates of life satisfaction.[3,4,5] A 2010 study found that college students with overinvolved parents were less open to new ideas, were more self-conscious, and were more likely to engage in drug use and other problem behaviors compared to kids with "free range" parents.[6]

reflection   In what ways have you made your children safer? How do you help them adapt to their challenging worlds? How would you know if you were behaving in an overprotective way?

In the end, our children never turn out the way we plan. Plenty of spiritual stories illustrate this fact, from the prodigal son to the historical Buddha. Let's look at the Buddha—Siddhartha Gautama—who was born into royalty to the ultimate helicopter parents. Before Siddhartha was even born, an oracle foretold that he would either become a renowned political leader or a spiritual figure. Of course, his father hoped for the former option, so Siddhartha's parents created an elaborate bubble of safety and comfort around the boy. They showered him with every pleasure, comfort, and delight. They also forbid him to leave the confines and safety of his gated community.

Still, the young man grew curious about what happened outside the palace walls. He convinced a servant to take him into the city and quickly encountered a world of profound suffering. During Siddhartha's first trip to the city, he saw a helpless and frail old man. On the next trip, he encountered a sickly and depressed man. On the third, he met a grieving family carrying a loved one's corpse. Siddhartha was baffled by each encounter, and he began to reflect on the suffering of inevitable old age, illness, and death. Eventually, the young prince decided to do something about it. He left the palace for good, renounced his status and his stuff, and became a wandering ascetic. If you know the story, you'll remember that total renunciation didn't work out so great for Siddhartha either. Only by following a middle path did he become enlightened.

We can almost imagine the privileged child brought from the gated community by his nanny into her neighborhood, only to be shocked awake by what he encountered. Or perhaps we know the sheltered child who heads off to a college or abroad only to return home a campus radical, renouncing his parents and upbringing, but then settling into a middle path by middle age. (Or maybe I'm just remembering my own younger self.)

The Buddha's story holds a lot of life lessons, but let's look at the most useful message for us parents: no matter how hard we try, our kids must and will forge their own paths, and despite our best intentions to protect them, they will eventually encounter suffering. But how they meet challenges and obstacles—whether they fight or flee or embrace and transform—is somewhat up to us. We can't defend them from every pain that's coming their way, but we can—and must—prepare them with the tools they'll need to face the world. What would the world look like if our greatest spiritual teachers or philosophers had never encountered suffering?

reflection   What's your style of parenting? What are the moments in which you are most likely to overparent? What about underparenting? What would a middle way between those two look like for you, and how could you aim for it?

What does the middle path look like between creating a safer world and producing a savvy, resilient, street-smart kid? As with most things, it's not a matter of *more* effort and energy but *right* effort and energy. This presents a challenge, of course, because our kids—and the world—are constantly growing and changing. As a guideline, I've adapted the "5 W's and H" of journalism—who, what, where, why, when, and how (though I leave out "where" below). To begin with, let's look at the reasons we want to engage in right effort in the first place.

Why?

What's our intention here? In short, it's not just about saving energy; it's also about giving our kids the best chance of growing up happy and resilient. There are four reasons to commit ourselves to right effort: first, to diminish unhelpful states of mind (depression, anxiety, confusion); second, to heal those states when they arise; third, to encourage positive states of mind (happiness, peace, resilience); and, lastly, to maintain these states as best we can. Most parents I know would love to pass on these four results to their children, but the motives beneath our choices don't always reflect this desire.

While past generations may have underparented, leaving us with thousands of hours of therapy, our generation is more likely to fall in the overparenting trap, missing the mark on the middle path of what I've heard called "benevolent neglect." Overparenting may involve mixed motives, but we also do it because it makes our life easier when we don't have to deal with the tantrum that results from a *no*. Sometimes our own self-image is caught up in how others (classmates, teachers, etc.) view our children, and this tempts us to touch up that science fair project. Other moments, we keep kids away from the dangers that we ourselves fear. Psychologist Madeline Levine points out three common patterns of overparenting: when we do something for our kids that they are already capable of doing, when we do something that they can almost do for themselves, and when we do something that has more to do with our own egos or, I might add, our own baggage.[7] It's important to check in every so often and ask ourselves *why* we do what we do and who is really benefitting.

How?

This is a big one. Even if we get our intentions on track, it doesn't mean we automatically know how to parent with right energy and effort.

At my first job out of college, I worked as a special education teacher at a residential school for kids with severe emotional problems. I was an English major; I'd never taken an education class in my life. Needless to say, I felt overwhelmed by my experiences with the kids and thoroughly confused by all the policies and procedures we had to follow. One coworker—a genial, if jaded, veteran special education teacher—saw my struggle and said (in a thick Boston accent): "Chris, to do this job and not make yourself crazy, you gotta figure out how to work *smahtah, not hahdah*." That maxim has stayed with me in work and parenting as a practical definition of right effort. So, to avoid overparenting and exhausting yourself, parent smarter, not harder.

Those of you who have practiced meditation are familiar with this principle. You have to use just the right amount of energy to nudge your mind back to some kind of clear, peaceful anchor. If you try too hard, you'll exhaust yourself, make your body tense and sore, or get a headache; if you don't try hard enough, you'll space out, make grocery lists in your head, or simply fall asleep. One ancient analogy refers to tuning an instrument—not too tight, not too loose. Practicing smarter in this context means finding just the right amount of effort for you in your particular circumstance—a guideline that can be applied directly to your parenting. Ideally, finding that balance point looks like what positive psychologist Mihály Csíkszentmihályi labels *flow*—that sweet spot when a task challenges us but keeps us happily engaged.[8]

Your balance point as a family most likely looks different from mine, but most families benefit from some degree of predictability or rhythm. Predictability saves us effort in the long run and helps kids feel safer and adults feel saner. In addition, as Kim John Payne (author of *Simplicity Parenting*) points out, when we establish rhythm and routine in our families, it allows us to occasionally break routines while paradoxically reinforcing them.[9] For example, if your kids normally go to bed at eight but vacation means they get to stay up later, that break in routine actually reinforces the particular rhythm of the school year. Or when your children encounter different sets of rules around screen time at a friend's house, it helps your kids learn to cope with different experiences they will invariably meet in the world. That being said, I highly recommend establishing routines with your kids in the morning (to get their brains ready for a busy day) and at night (to comfort them and help them relax and reflect). Regardless of what you choose to do, remember that consistency and predictability are important—they help your kids become attached in a healthy way and foster their ability to regulate their emotions and reactions to changes later on.

Working smarter (not harder) often comes down to paying attention to our behavior and simply cutting out some of the ways we overparent. Here's a fun exercise: grab a sheet of paper and quickly list the first ten things you do for your child on a daily basis (if you're like me, you might need more than one piece of paper). Here's an example from a day with my son:

1. Wake up when I hear Leo cry.

2. Get out of bed and go to him.

3. Pick Leo up and soothe him.

4. Change his diaper.

5. Change his clothes.

6. Get a bottle of milk.

7. Try to make coffee while preventing Leo from climbing the bookshelf.

8. Try to drink coffee while preventing Leo from stealing my phone and throwing it in the trash again (maybe he's on to something?).

9. Play with Leo intermittently while also trying to fold laundry (mostly his) and wash dishes (also mostly his).

10. Prepare breakfast for Leo and try to convince him to eat it.

Okay, so those are my first ten things, and I haven't even made it through breakfast yet, to say nothing of my own breakfast. As Leo gets older, he'll be able to do more on his own, of course. He'll feed himself, dress himself, and not practice death-defying bookcase climbs in the blink of an eye, though he will certainly find other, more worrisome death-defying behaviors out of sight. In the meantime, we'll still be tempted, like all other parents, to clean up after him, prepare his meals, and intervene when interactions with friends go awry.

Before those tween and teen years kick in, what can we do to help our kids develop independence and prepare for the world? Take a look at your list and ask yourself which things you can start to let go of now. What freedom can you offer everyone in the family by teaching your children the real-world skills they need to acquire?

In my work, I've been surprised that an increasing number of kids have yet to get their driver's licenses. I know several high school seniors and even college kids who have become so comfortable being driven around by their parents or others that they have never bothered to obtain their license, and now they feel too anxious about the responsibility that driving entails. Having been a kid who couldn't wait to drive, I've been baffled by this. Who wouldn't want the freedom and autonomy that come from having your own license?

To me, this reluctance symbolizes a larger trend. When we do too much for them, kids grow up believing they aren't capable of doing things on their own, whether it's learning to drive or completing their homework. At worst, kids feel like they have no control and end up with a sense of "learned helplessness"—the idea that they have no influence over anything in their lives. This leads to anxiety and depression and crushes intrinsic motivation.

But there's good news: our kids can rise to the occasion. If they learn in an age-appropriate way, small children love to be helpful around the house. As they get older, kids feel important when we ask them to hold the screwdriver while doing some repairs around the house, to look up directions when we get lost, or to lead a gratitude practice before meals. Ideally, we find the middle path for our family between over- and underparenting, challenging our children in just the right amount and offering just enough structure that they're able to learn for themselves.

If you're not sure what constitutes an age-appropriate task for your child, I strongly recommend the work of Lindsay Hutton of the Family Education Network.[10] I've adapted some of her advice here to give you a brief rundown:

Ages 2 to 3: Small Chores and Basic Grooming

This is the age when your children will start to learn basic life skills.
By the age of three, your children should be able to

- help put toys away and clean up spills;

- dress themselves with some help;

- put dirty clothes in the hamper and put trash and recycling in their proper places;

- help with setting and clearing the table for meals;

- wash up and brush teeth with some assistance; and

- help with the care of younger siblings.

Ages 4 to 5: Important Names and Numbers

When your children reach this age, safety skills are a priority.

By this age, your children should

- know the full name, address, phone number, and emails of important people;

- know how to make an emergency call;

- engage in simple cleaning chores, like sweeping or pet care;

- recognize cash denominations and have at least a vague sense of their value;

- perform basic hygiene independently (brushing hair and teeth, washing up);

- pick out clothes to wear; and

- ask doctors, waitstaff, teachers, and tour guides their own questions, with some assistance.

Ages 6 to 7: Basic Chores

Kids at this age can start to help with cooking meals and helping around the house.

Have your kids

- mix, stir, and cut ingredients, with supervision;

- make a basic meal, such as a sandwich;

- help put the groceries away;

- wash the dishes and empty the dishwasher;

- make the bed without assistance;

- bathe with minimal supervision;

- make some of their own purchasing decisions, with parental guidance;

- write their own thank-you notes; and

- complete homework and chores with prompting and checking.

Ages 8 to 9: Taking Care of Things

By this time, your children should take pride in their personal belongings and take care of them properly.

By this age, your children should be able to

- fold clothes;

- learn simple repairs, with supervision of tools, glue, or sewing equipment;

- take care of outdoor toys such as a bike or roller skates;

- perform personal hygiene without prompting;

- vacuum and sweep;

- read a recipe and prepare a simple meal;

- bathe unsupervised;

- help with the grocery list and shopping;

- understand how to save and budget their
  money and to count and make change;

- help with outdoor chores, such as watering and weeding;

- take out the trash and recycling;

- get homework and chores done, with minimal
  input and checking over from you;

- learn to use a calendar and manage and
  plan time with supervision;

- shovel snow and scrape ice from car; and

- resolve some peer and sibling conflicts
  with parental guidance.

Ages 10 to 13: Gaining Independence

Ten is about the age when your children can begin to perform many skills independently.

Your children should know how to

- stay home alone safely;

- walk to the store to make small purchases;

- change bedsheets;

- do laundry and dishes;

- plan and prepare a meal using the oven;

- learn to use basic hand tools, with supervision;

- change lightbulbs;

- mow the lawn;

- look after younger siblings or neighbors;

- use a calendar and budget time for small tasks effectively;

- begin to arrange play dates and plan their own social life and free time;

- begin chores and homework unprompted; and

- ask teachers and school staff for help.

Ages 14 to 18: More Advanced Skills

By the age of fourteen, your children should master all of the previous skills. On top of that, they should also be able to

- perform more sophisticated cleaning and maintenance chores, such as changing the vacuum cleaner bag, cleaning the stove, and unclogging drains;

- fill a car with gas and fill and change tires;

- understand food labels and basic nutrition;

- read and understand medicine labels and dosages;

- interview for, get, and keep a job;

- prepare and cook meals;

- plan their own transportation needs;

- manage time effectively, including planning and making appointments, with some guidance;

- resolve conflicts with adults, with your guidance; and

- understand and budget their own finances, including learning about the risks and benefits of checking accounts and credit cards.

Young Adults: Preparing to Live on Their Own

Your children will need to know how to support themselves when they go away to college or move out.

By now, they should know how to

- make regular doctor and dentist appointments and other important health-related appointments independently;

- schedule oil changes and perform other basic car maintenance;

- have a basic understanding of finances and be able to manage a bank account, balance a checkbook, pay bills, and possibly obtain and use a credit card, with some assistance;

- understand basic contracts, such as for an apartment or car lease;

- understand how to use health insurance; and

- pay some or all of their own bills.

The key to not helicoptering is to line up developmental abilities with appropriate tasks, instruct kids as needed, and talk about the activities. This list might not be exactly right for your family, and your kids won't always be thrilled about learning to do more for themselves, but you can link the new responsibilities with new freedoms. Also, keep in mind that having kids help around the house isn't just about making your life easier (especially when the food they prepare takes twice as long and comes with twice the mess). Ultimately, it's about making a wise, long-term investment. Teaching your kids self-reliance means a more meaningful form of liberation for everyone in the family.

reflection   Which items on this list jump out at you? Which will be particularly hard for your children to learn? Which tasks will be particularly difficult for you to let go of? Which do you look forward to letting go of?

Who?

This may seem like a simple question to answer. After all, you are the parent. But consider how much we outsource the care and supervision of our children—their education, after-school activities, health care, and so much more. There's no shame in this, of course. As the adage goes, it takes a village to raise a child.

My wife and I had only been parents for a few months when we had brunch with some friends of ours—seasoned parents in their own right. We commiserated and compared notes about catching colds, finding childcare, and dealing with the lack of sleep that comes with having an infant. "Wait a minute," our friend Rachel interrupted. "You were *both* up when Leo was crying? Total rookie move. No wonder you're both exhausted. You have to take turns, or you'll end up killing each other!"

There's something irreplaceably special about those first few months with your newborn child. The weeks race by in a blur. I don't want to discourage anyone from maximizing that precious and (relatively) brief period, but our friends' advice on balance will prove invaluable as your kids age. If there are two or more caregivers, find ways to balance the workload and delegate so as not to exhaust yourself. When your kids are babies, take shifts or alternate nights; as they grow older, consider the big picture and share responsibilities of rides, meals, and everything else.

With some social progress, we can have more productive conversations about who is responsible for what and when. We can split things down the middle at 50/50. However, with two busy careers, it might help to have more give-and-take on a daily basis or for even larger spans of time. A wonderful article by Andrew Moravcsik in *The Atlantic* discusses "lead parenting"—taking turns with which parent leads at home and which leads in career.[11] It's a helpful construct, especially in a marriage of two ambitious adults. My wife and I tend to take the lead on different weekend days or when we travel, alternating the role of "Family Activities Director." As I'm writing this paragraph, I'm in London taking care of my son while my wife works—I've taken off most of the summer from my clinical practice. I spend the mornings with Leo and write during his afternoon naps. At other times of the year, the balance changes in our family, as it will at other points in our life together.

At some point as parents, our kids enter "the village." They are parented along the way by teachers, coaches, music instructors, and maybe even therapists. This form of sharing responsibilities can be a relief, but it also can be painful or even threatening. I often encounter parents who are clearly concerned that I am somehow "better" at communicating with their children than they are. But my work with their kids is always temporary. Keep in mind that children—especially adolescents—*need* someone outside the family to offer a safe sounding board so they can then reconnect with their family. And most kids return to their own family's values after a period of searching or rebelling, even if it's not a whole Rumspringa. This process is full of ups and downs, but I'm reminded by older parents that there's light at the end of the tunnel.

In a recent support group for parents, a mother of a successfully launched young adult encouraged us all by saying, "Just wait. Keep connecting with your children, try to stay calm, and think of the long view. The cards you'll get for Mother's Day and Father's Day when they're twenty-five are totally worth the wait." I hope my own parents would agree.

 reflection   How do you and your co-parent share the lead with parenting? Which roles would you like to change or adapt over time? What other adults in your child's life can they connect with when things are difficult at home?

When?

Simply put, catch it early. The best time to make an effort is before the problem happens—"Put things in order before they arise," as Lao-Tzu reportedly instructed. Whether this is teaching our teens how to rotate the tires before they get a flat or having "that" conversation with our tweens before they become sexually active, it's our job as parents to prepare our children for the world they'll face before any of us are ready. Think about it, we teach kids fire safety and practice drills, hoping they'll never have to use them. On a less dramatic note, we can preview difficult confrontations with peers or teachers, nervous first days of school or summer camp, and managing forbidden or frightening foods at a friend's house. Talking and visualizing their way through anticipated difficulties—a process known as *elaborative rehearsal*—helps kids feel confident in new situations and builds strong executive functioning. As you might recall, chapter 4 also discusses previewing and reviewing.

As kids become teens, it's a good idea to keep this previewing and reviewing casual. With my adolescent patients, I ask, usually at the end of our sessions, "Any good stuff coming up in the next week?" Asking in this seemingly offhand manner, rather than in a mechanical way, invites reflection and previewing, even when teens grunt some indecipherable, monosyllabic answer. For younger kids, you can have fun and play a bit more. For years, my mom sang me "The Tomorrow Song" (the same song her father sang to her), previewing the next day's events. It went something like this:

> *Tomorrow is Tuesday.*
> *You'll get up, have breakfast, get dressed, and go to school.*
> *It's a cold day, so you'll need a coat.*
> *You have gym and library, so pack your books and shoes.*
> *Laura will walk you home, and you can have a snack and*
>   *play outside.*
> *Daddy will be home by four . . .*

The song went on and on. When my mom forgot a detail about the coming day, I would remind her, and we would add it to the song. As I grew older, we sang the song less and less, but the practice of previewing the coming day remained.

When can also refer to predictability and rhythm, which—as I've emphasized before—are important for kids. But we don't have to be rigid to help our children feel safe and regulated. *Roughly* the same rhythm of days and weeks is good enough, though a more predictable rhythm is preferable with kids who have executive function issues. Some schools these days operate six days of the week, which makes me (not to mention their parents) crazy. How are these kids supposed to align with the rest of the world's five-day week?

When can also mean knowing the right time for a challenging conversation. That means knowing when our kids are the most open and calm—maybe it's during a car ride, when taking a walk in the woods, or while doing chores side by side. Staring each other down as you discuss a challenging topic will be tough for both of you (I learned that early on as a therapist); it's more effective to talk while *doing* something side by side (a puzzle, game, drawing) and simply bringing up topics as you go. We (men, in particular) are wired to feel threatened in that eye-contact-directly-across-from-each-other stance; it tends to make our "upstairs" brains shut down. The path of least resistance into that prefrontal cortex is when our kids feel safe, are well fed and rested, and are not too stressed or emotional about anything else.

reflection   When are the best times to hold important or difficult conversations with your kids? What helps them feel more open and relaxed?

What?

What do we choose to focus our efforts on? What do we choose to let go of? These are some of the hardest questions of parenthood—deciding which battles to fight and which to let go. What's more, this conundrum often creates conflict with our co-parents. You might be a stickler for "please" and "thank you," while your partner is more worried about dirty hands and messy rooms. Remember, you don't have to solve every problem or challenge all at once, just as you aren't obligated to show up for every argument you are invited to.

We can counter the *what* problem to a degree by limiting choices for our kids. Parents often are tempted to offer unlimited options (maybe because they have trouble deciding for themselves). But as we learned in chapter 3, too many choices can paralyze kids or lead to rumination and regret about whether they made the right choice. So make everyone's life easier by offering fewer (or no) options, especially at younger ages. Little kids don't even have the prefrontal lobes to effectively make complex choices. Too much choice overtaxes the prefrontal cortex and limits resources for self-control, patience, ethical decision making, and other important functions,[12] potentially leading to more meltdowns, not fewer. So, you actually empower your kids when you limit their choices—what economists call *choice architecture*. For example, "Do you want to take your bath before or after dinner?" is better than "When do you want your bath?" and leads to them thinking they chose the bath. As a client I work with in sales says, "Never give the customer an opportunity for a no."

reflection What battles can you let go of, at least for now? How can you streamline or reduce your kids' choices? Are there points with your partner where you struggle with different priorities?

Here's another tip: according to a study by researcher Ellen Langer, when you want your kids to do something, the *way* you ask matters. People are more likely to agree to a request or an instruction when you offer a reason (even a nonsensical one).[13] Rather than telling your kid to "Set the table," you'll find more success if you try something like, "Set the table because it's dinner time."

Another big "what" in terms of perennial battles is around food. Resistence to eating new foods may even be hardwired in by evolution. But there's good news: before age five, kids may not eat balanced meals, but within the span of seven days, many will eat a balanced *week's* worth of food. While they may refuse vegetables one night at dinner, they can learn to listen to their bodies and find those needed nutrients in the next well-rounded meal we place in front of them. We can also invest effort in the short run and save in the long run by involving our kids not in making choices but in making food—from gardening to slicing and stirring, each step of the way leads to more ownership over the meal. We don't know for certain whether children were historically picky eaters, but we do know they probably helped at all these stages of the meal and were less picky in the past. We can also encourage them to try every food ten times before giving up, which also leads to fewer blanket pronouncements of "dislike." So with spinach, that means spinach salad, sautéed spinach, saag paneer, spanakopita, spinach quiche, spinach pasta, and so on. Wouldn't it be a relief to have your kids say they dislike half of these items rather than a blanket refusal of spinach? My friend Mark Bertin, a developmental pediatrician, is adamant about not making "kid food," which takes more effort and sends the message that kid food and adult food are different things, discouraging experimentation. He also recommends putting everything on a kid's plate. Even if they just eat the burrito wrapper today, eventually they will eat the insides. But they never will if they don't first get used to it being on their plate.

When we can find a middle path between under- and overparenting, it's incredible how much we can help our families. We'll often miss the mark, but we can keep getting closer, moving to one side or the other depending on our situations, histories, and temperaments. This is also where our self-compassion helps. We feel tremendous shame and anxiety about over- or underparenting, and we judge ourselves preemptively before the other playground parent, professional, or even our partner has a chance to. Let the unhelpful comparisons go.

On a flight across the Atlantic recently, Leo got his first exposure to screen time (he even tried to hug Daniel Tiger through the iPad). While we could have spent six hours exhausting ourselves trying to entertain him without screens, it felt like "right effort" to let him watch Daniel Tiger for a while. After all, we had jet lag and the stresses of being in a foreign country to look forward to, and it wasn't like we wouldn't watch movies had we been flying without him. In the end, what was the point? So do your best. It won't always be the perfect choice, but you can usually steer yourself toward some relief for you and your family.

You don't have to be perfect, and neither do your children. Freud and the early psychoanalysts were notoriously misogynistic mother-blamers, and we still carry a lot of their bias with us. More recently, however, child analysts have lightened up, so to speak. D. W. Winnicott, for example, stresses that kids don't need a perfect parent; that parent just has to be "good enough."[14] You don't have to clothe your baby in organic, locally sourced, hand-sewn diapers that are only washed in a Himalayan stream by unionized Tibetan refugees. Just do your best. All you need to be is a "good enough" parent. Love your imperfect self and love your imperfect family.

Reminders and Reflections

- By the time they reach college, kids with overinvolved parents tend to be more self-conscious and more likely to engage in problem behaviors like drug use.

- Previews and reviews, predictability, and rhythm help your children feel safer.

- What are your signs to know if you were under- or overparenting?

- What are ways in which you can parent smarter, not harder?

- What things that you do for your child can you let go of or teach them to do?

- Remember Shantideva's words and don't try to coat the world in leather. Don't spend your energy trying to make the world perfectly safe. Protect your kids while teaching them to protect themselves.

- Find ways to share the "lead parent" role at different stages in your own and your children's lives.

- Consider streamlining some of the choices you offer your kids.

- Pick your battles, and don't show up to every fight you're invited to.

- Remember that you don't have to be perfect, just "good enough."

CHAPTER 6

the buddha
and the marshmallow

(Raising Patience—Khanti)

Most of us feel like we need more patience. I'd even bet that patience, as a quality, tops almost any parent's wish list. If you think you have enough patience, then feel free to skip to the next chapter (on, ahem, *honesty*). For those of you still reading, here's some good news: as with all the paramis, patience, like a muscle, comes with practice, and it only develops in situations where you need it. That's extra-good news for those of us who feel like our children (or spouses or jobs) regularly "try" our patience. The bad news is that we can't expect our kids to develop patience unless we embody it ourselves.

Patience in Spirituality and Science

Nearly every spiritual tradition has a tale demonstrating the virtues of patience and forbearance. Remember the story I told of the Buddha's life in chapter 5? After renouncing his life of luxury, Siddhartha lived for years as a wandering ascetic. Yet, despite all his sacrifice and spiritual practice, he still had not found an end to suffering. One day, exhausted and starving, the former prince plopped down beneath fig tree to rest and enjoy a snack that a young girl had offered to share. Realizing that neither his extreme self-sacrifice nor the self-indulgence of his childhood would bring the answers he sought, Siddhartha vowed to sit beneath the tree until he reached enlightenment.

And he did, but not without some torment trying his patience first. Mara—a powerful demon—had noticed that Siddhartha was about to achieve the ultimate spiritual goal, so the demon tempted him with riches, power, and pleasures—or whatever the sex, drugs, and rock-and-roll equivalents of 600 BCE were. Even so, the young man patiently sat through it all—unmoved and undistracted. Once the Buddha finally achieved enlightenment, Mara fled in a rage. This story echoes in the resistance of Job, Jesus, or Muhammad to Satan's temptations and torments. Patience is also extolled in classic literature and philosophy the world over. There's a good reason people throughout the ages have placed such a high value on perseverance and forbearance.

Social scientists have paid a lot of attention to patience, too. Walter Mischel, in his famous "marshmallow" study, investigated delayed gratification in young children, using a test for children that was perhaps even more devious than what Satan or Mara could devise.[1] Researchers left kids alone in a room with one marshmallow in front of them and gave them a challenge: if the kids could sit in the room for fifteen minutes without eating the marshmallow, they would be rewarded with *two* marshmallows. The children, unsurprisingly, displayed a range of reactions. A handful immediately grabbed the marshmallow, ate it, and that was that. Others were able to wait a few minutes before caving to the fluffy confectionary temptation. But a third group successfully made it through the longest fifteen minutes of a toddler's life to savor the hard-earned reward. How were these children able, like that young Siddhartha, to wait for their ultimate reward? Videos from the study show them covering their eyes, turning their chairs away from the marshmallows, and even pulling their hair to distract themselves. Some of the kids reported that they visualized the marshmallow as something less appealing. Others said they kept their minds unwavering on the reward at all times.

Why does it matter whether a four-year-old can resist a marshmallow for fifteen minutes? Mischel and his equally patient research team followed these "successful" kids into adulthood—they scored higher on SATs, had fewer discipline problems, and tended to enjoy more rewarding careers and relationships. According to Mischel, these kids were less likely to be arrested and more likely to have stable relationships, and, not surprisingly, they tended not to be obese.

Mischel and others have continued to study the causes and conditions under which we can and cannot delay gratification. Children from stable backgrounds with secure and trusting attachments are more able to delay, which makes sense. Why patiently wait for a marshmallow if the adult world has broken other promises? What if you have no idea where the next marshmallow will come from? The Buddha, too, felt safe when he sat down. Psychologist Rick Hanson points out that Siddhartha's back was to the tree, he was protected by the shade, and he just had a bite to eat, so his prefrontal cortex was better able stay on track.[2] If we consider the studies that indicate that children with parents who are overly controlling and "authoritarian," as well as children with negligent parents, struggle to delay gratification more than children with firm but forgiving "authoritative" parents, a middle path looks a lot more inviting.[3] Siddhartha's controlling parents caught a break on that one, or maybe his nanny was the wise adult figure in his life.

Happier, calmer, and wealthier kids are also more able to delay gratification, probably because they feel less desperate for a short-term fix. Stressed-out children struggle in particular. Hearing parents fight in the first year of life (even hearing parents fight while in the womb) can stress a child enough to have a negative impact.[4] When our son was only one-and-a-half years old, my wife and I were in a tense discussion about in-laws. We looked over to see Leo frozen with tension. We could also see his natural compassion arise when he ambled over and gave us a hug, reminding us to make peace with each other. Conflict isn't the end of the world, but remember how important it is for children to see that conflict resolved in a healthy way with order restored.

reflection   What makes it more difficult for your children to delay gratification? What triggers signal that you're about to "lose" your patience?

So what can a five-year-old staring down the temptation of a marshmallow tell us about ancient wisdom? What can ancient wisdom tell us about patience and self-discipline? How can we help our children resist not just the siren song of a marshmallow but all of the world's countless other temptations—from screens to sex to substances—over the course of a lifetime? Simply put, by recognizing our own "demons," we can calm the amygdala, activate our prefrontal cortex, and make a proactive strategy, rather than simply reacting to temptation.[5] Siddhartha recognized Mara as an illusion and fended off the demon with meditation, visualizations, and maybe even some chanting. The children in the marshmallow study used strategies that weren't too different—they sang songs, turned away, covered their eyes, tugged on their hair to focus on physical sensation, or kept their mind on the goal of that second marshmallow.

Here's one important takeaway: secure kids in the study were better able to invent a strategy and follow it through. We can help our children simply by giving them more security. We can also *teach* them visualization, distraction, and other techniques for keeping their eyes on the prize. To that end, here's a brief practice to try yourself or with your kids.

PRACTICE   The Marshmallow Meditation

As you read the following for the next minute or so, try not to think about a marshmallow (or, if marshmallows aren't your thing, pick your favorite dessert—a chocolate chip cookie, a red velvet cupcake, a scoop of strawberry ice cream). Do NOT think about that fresh fluffy marshmallow. Do NOT think about how spongy it is, and do NOT imagine the yummy powder that flakes off in your fingers. Do NOT imagine the sweet, slightly vanilla smell and its accompanying associations with summertime bonfires, cozy hot chocolate, or any other happy memories that arise. Do NOT think about the perfectly springy texture as you bite through the dry outside into the moist and sticky inside. Do NOT consider the sensation of the marshmallow bouncing with each bite you chew. And definitely do NOT feel your mouth watering as you raise the marshmallow to your lips and experience the sweet taste and texture as you bite into its soft squishy deliciousness.

Okay, you can stop now. Clear your head (and, if necessary, the corners of your mouth) and take a breath. Let's try the same exercise again, but this time I want you to read the same paragraph while feeling each in-breath and out-breath. When your mind wanders off into fantasy—say, on the glorious creaminess of the frosting on your unbelievably moist carrot cake—just remember your breath. Read a line or two and feel your in-breath. Read another couple of lines and really notice your out-breath. Okay, ready? Give it another go.

What was different this time around? Did you salivate less? Was the picture of the marshmallow (or other dessert) as sharp as before? How about the urge for a marshmallow? How does breathing in feel differently from breathing out? Practices like this can truly help us get through distractions and temptations, especially when they're coupled with a set determination to reach a specific goal, whether it be spiritual liberation, an A on the final exam, or just another marshmallow.

Cultivating Patience

Unfortunately, we don't live in a culture that promotes patience. With instant streaming movies, you no longer have to wait a year to watch the *Wizard of Oz*, to say nothing of occupying yourself for fifteen minutes after dinner waiting for *Mr. Rogers*. Microwaves ready dinner in five minutes, and home delivery of anything you could want arrives at the tap of an app. There's just not much of a need for patience these days, and that's no accident—if we could delay gratification, we wouldn't buy so much, or we might make healthier choices. Some might argue that these inventions make the ability to delay gratification obsolete, but consider that patience and delayed gratification correlate with emotional regulation, satisfying relationships, happiness, and lifelong resilience.

reflection   What (or who) helped you develop patience in your own childhood?

For decades, the beloved blue Cookie Monster on *Sesame Street* served as a comic demonstration of Freud's id, or what we might now think of as prefrontal failure. A few years back, the creators of *Sesame Street* consulted with Walter Mischel himself to offer Cookie Monster some patience strategies. In one sketch, game show host Guy Smiley offers Cookie Monster a similar choice to the Stanford subjects—one cookie now or two later. A chorus of "Waiting Game Singers" pop up to remind Cookie Monster of various strategies he can use to wait—singing to pass the time, visualizing the cookies inside a picture frame, playing with a toy, imagining the neutral aspects of the cookie like its shape and color, and pretending the cookie is a stinky fish. Mischel describes this process as shifting our brains from "hot" emotional focus to "cool" rational focus, or from amygdala to prefrontal cortex, helping us see the temptation as not real and thus removing the emotional and instinctual charge that makes it easier to delay gratification. One teacher I know uses the video and others like it to teach the marshmallow test to her second graders. The whole class even jokes about "Marshmallow moments"—times when it's a challenge to wait!

We certainly don't have to manufacture game shows or hire Guy Smiley to find situations to teach our kids to wait—the opportunities are all around us if we look. It was commonly accepted at my grandmother's house that you didn't eat until everyone was seated and my grandmother lifted her fork, and you didn't leave the table until you asked to be excused. That might seem old-fashioned, but there's a deep wisdom to manners such as these—it taught my siblings and I how to wait, if even for a minute or two. All we have to do, really, is slow down the instant-gratification train just a little—say a short blessing before meals, reserve brief times of day that are tablet- and smartphone-free, ask the kids to wait to speak while others are conversing, practice saying "not now" (while being sure to tell them *when* and suggesting an activity while they wait). By the way, asking our kids to "wait a minute" only works if they know how long a minute is, so my friend Bob suggests measuring time in breaths for younger children. Set a timer for one minute and have your child count how many breaths they take. This helps kids learn what "a minute" means and empowers them to feel successful in waiting.

For older children, get them involved in multistep projects. These require planning—which builds executive functioning—as well as communication skills, not to mention patience. Think of projects like ceramics, visual arts, carpentry, or even small home-improvement tasks that require following a series of instructions and plenty of planning ahead. Consider the planning and patience involved in baking and cooking—from the steps in making dough and then waiting for it to rise, then cook, then cool before eating. Gardening, taking care of plants, and looking after pets all build empathy, health, and happiness, not to mention patience and strong executive functions.[6] Solving puzzles and learning to play a musical instrument (or learning anything, for that matter) teach patience, determination, and how to tolerate frustration. Letting kids earn and save money also fosters patience, as they have to watch their account grow before they can buy that special something. It also gives them time to think about whether they really want or need it.

Patience can be fun. Think of all those observation games we played between rest stops on road trips as children—finding different license plates, counting cows, alphabet or word games, playing "I Spy," and more. So many games we don't bother playing any more like "Simon Says" or "Mother May I" teach valuable lessons like impulse control, waiting, and more. Use your own creativity to make up games together. Stuck in the aptly named *waiting room*? Invent funny names for everyone else slouched around you. Slow cashier at the grocery store? Make up crazy back-stories for everyone who walks by. Make a game of waiting—see who can walk the slowest, stay quiet the longest, or breathe the deepest breaths. Visualizing and play-acting are wonderful aids in this regard. Lev Vygotsky, a child development researcher, was able to make kids stand still four times as long when he had them imagine they were guards at a factory.[7]

Steal a page from the play therapy playbook by externalizing emotions—in this case, impatience—and draw pictures of the impatience demon (called *Impy*) or make puppets and act out plays that involve lots of "if-then" strategies for dealing with impatience. For example, "*If* Impy shows up while I have to wait for dessert, *then* I will imagine the cookies are rocks to fool Impy and make him go away!" Help your kids recognize all the times and places that Impy likes to show up (before dinner, in the car, at the post office) and what Impy feels like in their bodies (tingly, jumpy, jittery). Doing so brings their body and breath into the game to help them settle. They can also use their words ("I see you trying to trick me Impy, but I won't let you!"), which activates their prefrontal cortex, or more logical left brain. And don't forget to share your own impatience demon who pops up when you feel tired, just arrive home from work, or try to juggle too many things at once. Your Impy and theirs probably have a lot in common.

reflection   What strategies or games did you use as a kid for waiting and delaying gratification in line or on long car trips? What could your family come up with together to cultivate patience?

Time in nature is another way to appreciate slowness and learn to wait by checking in with our surroundings. A form of therapy popular in Japan and South Korea called Shinrin-yoku ("forest bathing") is essentially all about walking around the woods in silence. You might not have a forest nearby, but perhaps you can find a stream or river to watch for a lazy afternoon. Or get your kids to pay attention as "nothing" happens in the sky as clouds roll past. My first meditation practice was my father teaching me to make clouds disappear by focusing on them as I breathed steadily in and out. Later, as a teen, I went on a wilderness retreat that included a few days in the woods by myself. One of the guides gave me a tip that I still remember today: "Just go out and wait until you get bored, then wait some more until you get interested." As discussed in chapter 3, boredom is important cognitively; we miss out on its benefits when we're constantly caught up in too many high-tech distractions. Mother Nature is a wonderful antithesis to instant gratification (alongside teaching lessons in patience) as we watch how long she can patiently outwait human interference.

In the hilarious and incisive *Bringing Up Bébé*, Pamela Druckerman writes about what she calls *Le Pause*.[8] With *Le Pause*, French parents wait a moment before responding to a child's nighttime cry, giving the child a chance to learn how to comfort themselves. The length of this wait grows with the child, fostering patience in the child and the parents. I recently witnessed this in action when my friend Scott asked his four-year-old son to wait to look at pictures on his phone. He crouched to his son's level, connected with him, and explained, "Ezra, the grownups are looking at pictures now, then you can have your turn." Scott turned back to me and continued to show me the photos. Ezra's whining didn't stop entirely, but it subsided as his little brain calmed down and he exercised the waiting muscle. We enjoyed the pictures for a couple of minutes, then Scott rewarded his son with a "thank you," gave him validation for waiting, and let him view the photos himself.

We can begin by assuming that our children are capable of patience. Among other things, this assumption is far more respectful than believing (and conveying) that our kids just can't wait. Patience isn't like a light switch that's either on or off—we actually have to develop patience through trials over time. What's more, our patience is inextricably linked to that of our children. If our children grow impatient, often so do we, and vice versa. If we lose our patience and simply hand over whatever our kids want, we are not building anyone's ability to bear discomfort. The next time you're stuck in line somewhere, don't reach for your smartphone for entertainment (for you or your child); instead, try one of the activities suggested earlier or make up one of your own. Together, you and your children can build up those patience muscles.

Mindfulness, Awareness, and Compassion

Practicing mindfulness strengthens the prefrontal cortex and other parts of the brain associated with patience. When we slow down, pause, and reflect between activities, rather than rushing from one thing to the next, we not only give kids a chance to practice slowing down, but we also help them enjoy what they are doing more. Through mindfulness, we learn to be patient and compassionate with ourselves when the mind wanders again and again. Just as mindfulness builds patience, patience also builds mindfulness.

> PRACTICE   Inviting Impy (or Mara) to Play
>
> Take a few deep breaths and reflect on a time when you lost your patience recently. Where were you? Who were you with? In what ways were you feeling hungry, angry, lonely, or tired? What did the experience feel like in your body, mind, heart, and even your breath? Take a few deep breaths and try to call up the felt experience. What does it feel like now? Take a moment to send yourself some compassion and let the memory clear. After a minute or so of noticing your breath, reflect on a time when you exercised patience. What was that like? How did others respond? When you remember that experience in your body, how does it differ from the memory and associated sensations of impatience? After a few more breaths, let these images and feelings fade away, too.

It takes patience and practice to stay in the moment. Sometimes we are simply too hungry, angry, lonely, tired, or you-name-it to be patient. When these moments arise—and they will—do your best to practice some self-care. Ask for help if you can—all great leaders and spiritual leaders did and do. And just as I advised in the "When" section of chapter 5, do your best to catch things early. Know your own impatience triggers and those of your children, as well as your best skills, abilities, and rituals to fall back on. Validate and reinforce the moments when your kids effectively handle impatience and get curious—find out how they did it to help them build on their successes the next time Impy shows up. And if you or your kids give in to impatience, have some compassion (especially self-compassion).

reflection   Take a moment to reflect on a time when you were impressed with how well your children waited patiently. What strategies did they use? How can you help them access these techniques in the future?

You and your kids may never reach the point at which you want to befriend Mara or Impy, but you can extend the delay on gratification, handle boredom better, and become more patient. If this chapter is particularly meaningful to you or if you feel you need a little extra help, try repeating versions of the following short aspirational wishes before you fall asleep or the first thing in the morning. Research finds that when we make affirmations like "I am patient" and we aren't, we know we are lying to ourselves and feel worse. Try aspirational statements instead.

May I be patient.

May I learn to have patience.

May I learn to teach patience.

May my child be patient.

May my child learn to have patience.

May my child learn to offer patience.

Jean Piaget, the renowned Swiss researcher, often remarked on what he called the "American question."[9] Whenever he lectured in the United States on children's cognitive development, inevitably some parent would ask, "That's great, but how can we speed it up?" That is, how can we hasten the process of natural cognitive development? Despite our impatience, there aren't too many ways to speed up natural processes. You can't force a flower to bloom early; you can only create the conditions in which the flower might flourish. The same holds true with our kids. So be mindful of any unreasonable expectations you might have for your children and their current level of patience. We can't expect them to have the reflective and directive functioning of an adult, but we can certainly help them on their way.

At the end of his book on the marshmallow test, Mischel made a wise final point. We don't teach kids to delay gratification for its own sake. After all, a life without spontaneous marshmallows, or at least some sex and rock-and-roll, is hardly worth living. We teach kids patience so they can choose to use it or not. Freedom lies not in waiting but in having the choice to wait or not. Sometimes one marshmallow is better than two, especially if you can fully enjoy it in the moment.

Reminders and Reflections

- Strengthening patience requires practicing it in difficult-to-wait situations.

- It's a lot easier to deal with impatience when you're not hungry, angry, lonely, or tired.

- How do you model patience for your children?

- What patience-building multistep activities or hobbies can you encourage in your children?

- Use games, arts, nature, playful visualizations, and role-playing to help your kids wait and build their capacity.

- Practice *Le Pause*, connect, and offer a suggestion to help your children counter impatience.

- Make waiting an opportunity for observation of mindfulness.

- Recognize and reinforce your kids' patience strategies and build on those as they get older.

CHAPTER 7

what sets us free

(Raising Truthfulness—Sacca)

There are three things that cannot long be hidden:
the sun, the moon, and the truth.
THE BUDDHA

Truthfulness starts concretely—tell the truth; don't lie (this covers lies of omission, as well). This means telling the truth to ourselves and others, as well as encouraging truthfulness in future generations. When we tell our own truth wisely and ethically, especially spiritual or scientific truths, it can be an act of generosity and kindness, potentially liberating us all.

Why do we lie? Why do we tell the truth? When we are at our best—feeling safe, secure, and peaceful—honesty is easy. Yet study after study shows that when we are emotional, tired, or hungry, our moral muscles weaken, our prefrontal preventive measures fail, and we succumb to temptation and cheating.[1] This research indicates the importance of self-care in encouraging honesty and our best behavior.

The slippery slope effect is real. Dan Ariely's *The (Honest) Truth about Dishonesty* sums up much of the most recent compelling (and amusing) research on why we lie, cheat, and steal.[2] Even when dishonesty begins with a minor foible, it creates both inward and outward ripples. For example, a small "gateway" lie often leads to larger lies in what Ariely names the "What-the-Hell Effect." This effect occurs partially through social reinforcement and partially through us establishing new mental habits (and neural pathways) that crash through the safety barriers of our conscience and social contract. In fact, a recent study scanned the brains of people as they lied and discovered that with each successive lie, their limbic warning system reacted less and less.[3] Basically, the subjects were desensitizing themselves to dishonesty, leading them to lie more severely and more frequently.

Dishonest behaviors also spread outward through groups. Witnessing petty crimes has been shown to inoculate us, making it more likely that we will commit such crimes ourselves.[4] Cheating is especially contagious when we see people in our community do it (be it at school, on the team, or in the family) as opposed to when we see an outsider cheat. When we do cheat, we are more likely to invite others to join us, perhaps to soothe our guilty conscience and quiet that pesky cognitive dissonance that comes when we violate our own values. From here, it's easy to see how corruption spreads through once fair and supposedly meritocratic institutions—"What the Hell," indeed.

We are also more likely to act dishonestly if it benefits others, in a kind of "Robin Hood Effect." Consider this in relation to your own family—the white lies to get your child into a doctor's appointment early, the strings you pull to get your child into the right classroom, or the lengths you'd go to save your kids from trouble. This is perhaps the darker side of our inborn altruism. How often do we sacrifice our ethical integrity, even in small ways, for our family and friends? In what ways are our expectations of others stricter than the rules we apply to our loved ones or even ourselves?

Chapter 2 touched on the ways that ethics can help keep everyone safe. Dishonesty is bad for all of us—not only does it erode trust in a family or community, it also usually comes back to haunt us as individuals. We experience the stresses and cognitive dissonance of repeating the lie, telling more cover-up lies, and trying to remember how all the untruths fit together. When we don't speak authentically, when we don't present our "truth" to others, we are reinforced in not being ourselves, trapping us in a maze of false facades that don't match who we really are.

What's more, when we behave dishonestly, research shows that we are more likely to view others and the world as dishonest, untrustworthy, and unpleasant,[5] which is almost the textbook definition of depression. One of the most quoted lines in the *Dhammapada* (a sacred Buddhist text) asserts, "As we think and act, so our world becomes." When we think and act dishonestly, our outlook sours, and we live in a darker and less trustworthy world. Essentially, dishonesty furthers our anxiety, depression, isolation, and negative outlook.

The fact is, we don't live in a world where everyone is honest. Thus, it would be foolish to teach our children to be naively trusting of others. But we can teach them a healthy skepticism. Some kids—especially those from difficult backgrounds—already approach the world with a street-smart type of suspicion appropriate to the kind of world they will likely be entering. A more privileged child can afford to trust in a way that a child from an unstable background cannot, which is one reason people who have experienced trauma or other violations of trust may struggle with attachment, depression, and anxiety. For kids with these experiences, helping them feel safe (by being a trustworthy adult) teaches them to begin to trust the world again and learn to thrive.

reflection   What explicit and implicit lessons do you teach your children about trusting others and trusting the world? How do you help them determine truth from falsehood?

Telling the Truth to Ourselves and the World

How do we tell the truth to ourselves and to the world? To begin with, we must look clearly at our own thoughts and behavior. We might ask whether the old stories we tell about ourselves, others, and the world—the stories we use to justify our own behavior—are actually true. Our minds show a "confirmation bias," which is that funny habit of rewriting the past to fit our preexisting views and biases. If our children get disciplined at school, do we jump to blame their teachers or friends, or do we hold ourselves (and them) accountable? Sometimes we have to confront or speak some painful truths: Our child may need more help than we can provide. We may need to seek therapeutic, academic, or medical support. Or we may require a drastic change in our relationship with our partners, family, or friends. Honesty often requires tremendous courage.

Telling the truth to others really can set us free, which is why therapy, confession, and counseling groups are so effective. That hardly means telling every parent in the PTO our darkest secret, nor does it mean going into detail about the textures and colors we found in our newborn's diaper when talking with a colleague at the water cooler. But it does mean we need to open up to others skillfully.

Speaking honestly and unburdening yourself of pain and past hurt can even be an act of kindness to yourself and others, especially those who have experienced similar pain. When we share skillfully, we see we are not alone in our suffering. When we talk about our fear of being bad parents in a new parent support group, we connect to others with compassion. When we share the truth of our own childhood struggles in an appropriate way with our own child, we practice generosity. When we speak honestly about supporting a child through mental illness or addiction, we offer wisdom and hope to another suffering parent. As a therapist and workshop facilitator, I witness this all the time. Remember from chapter 3—just putting words to our pain rewires our brains to integrate those experiences in healthy ways.

Just as dishonesty has a ripple effect, so does honesty. Speaking our truth and teaching our children to speak theirs has a powerful effect, empowering others in a virtuous cycle. We see this when one brave soul names an injustice, thus giving courage to more survivors and allies to speak up—whether it's about defeating the stigma of illness or the silencing of sexual assault survivors, addressing systems of oppression, or raising a child who is noticeably "different" from his or her peers. Oppression and shame thrive on isolation and secrecy; speaking our truth is the path back into the world. Suffering is universal, and many would argue it is what makes us human. Your truth can help others more than you may realize, while your silence may unwittingly reinforce their isolation.

None of this is easy. It takes courage to speak your truth—whether to those who have hurt you or to those who love you (even when they are the same person). We encounter these moments when we confront a relative's casual racism, let an irresponsible babysitter go, or confront our spouse about a thorny issue in our relationship.

reflection Which of your stories about the world might not be entirely true? What makes it difficult for you to speak up and tell the truth to others?

Use Your Words: Skillfully Telling and Encouraging the Truth

We all say things we don't mean in the heat of the moment. Still, we can cause lasting damage when we make threats we can't keep or tell our children that they're spoiled or say "you'll never understand" to our partner. The more we speak unskillfully, the more we create a world that reflects how we think and act. If we tell our son that he is bratty, we will come to see him that way. If we tell our partner they will never understand us, we will both give up trying to understand.

However, if we can stay calm, compassionate, and connected, we can more easily speak the truth effectively. "You're a spoiled brat" becomes "You are acting entitled right now"—the latter isn't quite as likely to shut your child down or create a fixed mindset in either of you (more on this in chapter 8). You could also choose to make an "I" statement, such as "I'm feeling taken for granted right now" or "I don't feel we're understanding each other right now." These feelings are inevitable in any relationship, and this type of "I" statement is much more likely to be heard and more effective than using the language of blame and accusation. Of course, it can be frightening to be vulnerable in this way, but it serves all of us to find honest, skillful ways to speak our truth and to ask for what we need.

We can encourage truthfulness in our children by skillfully using language. For example, when it comes to cheating in sports or school, telling kids to not be "cheaters" may be more effective than telling them "don't cheat." Although many of us can justify cheating here and there, no one wants to consider themselves a "cheater." In the past, many thought it was only struggling students who cheated; nowadays, it's competitive college-bound students who are most likely to do so. According to a fact sheet from Stanford University, between 75 and 98 percent of college students reported that they had cheated in high school.[6] There is also strong evidence that honor codes actually work to some degree; signed pledges at the beginning of paperwork or an exam (rather than at the end) may be most effective.[7]

Slippery Slopes

To put myself through graduate school, I tutored high school students. I vividly remember one father—a high-powered surgeon—saying as he interviewed me, "I'm sick of writing my kid's damn papers. I've heard you're good. Can you help him?" I patiently explained that I could certainly help his son write his papers, but that I wouldn't write them for him. I spent a few dozen hours working with the sweet sixteen-year-old, helping him research, outline, and ultimately write a ten-page paper on the Trail of Tears. He finished it, bibliography and all, and felt proud at having done the work himself (for once). His first independent performance earned a B from his teacher; my performance got me fired by his dad. While not many of us would go so far as writing our kids' papers for them, who hasn't been tempted to touch up our child's work before they hand it in?

And what are we to do when it seems like every other parent is, at a minimum, touching things up? It's undeniable that not bending the rules may put our kids at some disadvantage. But we need to consider the long-term effects on their work ethic and self-esteem. One young woman I saw in therapy cheated just a little bit on her assignments. Her classmates, teachers, and parents saw her as gifted, but the fact that *she* knew she was cheating was slowly corroding her sense of self-worth, which led her to sneak vodka every night from her parents' liquor cabinet. The gap between how others saw her and how she saw herself was increasingly unbearable. Eventually, the chasm of cognitive dissonance became too painful, and she allowed herself to get caught cheating (which also stopped her nightly drinking). While the admission was painful for her, it relieved the pressure she was placing on herself. In the long run, it also stopped the cycle of dishonesty about who she was and how she presented herself to the world. It may have also prevented potential substance problems down the road.

reflection   What would you do to help your child "get ahead"? How might other parents in your community answer that question?

Cheating is hardly a victimless crime that ends with us—it's a contagion. It does not end with the classmate who cheats; it actually spreads from there, passing the ethical dilemma to the next student and the next, until someone finally makes the difficult decision to stop. The good news is that the opposite is also true. While it may not feel good to be the only family not gaming the system, your family will be in a happier, stronger place in the long run. Trust that the hard-won honesty will spread. Even if it doesn't turn the tide, it will at least slow it, bettering the world your child will inhabit.

Lao-Tzu's "put things in order before they arise" approach is important here, too. There will come a day when you can no longer pick your child's playmates, but when they are young, you can make informed decisions about a good number of the kids and adults in their lives. It took me a while to realize that the wisest way to choose a nursery school is not just by getting to know the teachers and curriculum but also by getting to know the other families. The same holds true for those of us who can afford to choose the community where we live.

Cultivating Honesty in Our Children

When we catch our child lying for the first time, it can be heartbreaking. Unfortunately, it's an inevitable part of parenthood. For toddlers, the ability to get what they want develops before their moral compass does, which makes some evolutionary sense. In fact, lying can be a sign of maturity, intelligence, and even social development.[8]

I still recall feeling like a proud Papa when I gazed at my eight-month-old's empty tray of pasta and cauliflower. *My son is such an amazing eater*, I thought to myself. *He's going to eat everything and grow up to be a real foodie, just like his parents* (ignoring the fact that "eating everything" at that time also included rocks, grass, and his cousin's toys). Plucking him from his high chair to give him a kiss before texting my wife the good news, I looked down only to notice that he'd managed to stuff all the cauliflower into the sides of his highchair. Fortunately, this doesn't mean I'm the terrible father of a budding sociopath—30 percent of three-year-olds will lie or cheat if they think they can get away with it, and by age four, this percentage increases to 80 percent. The average four-year-old lies every two hours, and by age six, hourly![9]

Most of these untruths from our young children are small cover-ups, but we need to be mindful of how we respond, because punishment can inadvertently reinforce dishonesty. It's likely that our kids will keep lying because they don't want to disappoint us with the initial crime. Therefore, our energy is best expended when we address the cover-up lie (to teach them about honesty), as well as the crime or accident they're attempting to cover (if it's important).

If lying comes to us so naturally and so early, how can we hope to teach honesty? In the past, we relied a lot on fables, though to mixed results. One study actually compared *The Boy Who Cried Wolf* with *Pinocchio* and the legend of six-year-old George Washington cutting down the cherry tree ("I cannot tell a lie"). Most of us might guess that of these, the tragic tale of *The Boy Who Cried Wolf* would be most effective in diminishing dishonesty. In fact, the more positive George Washington tale reduced lying by 75 percent in boys and 50 percent in girls, whereas the other two stories made no difference.[10]

Why might that be? Harshly punishing the lie—whether taking away dessert or becoming dessert for the wolf—unwittingly teaches that dishonesty is *bad for the child* as opposed to *bad for the community*. When we react to our kids' lying with harsh punishment, research tells us it merely sets the stage to make children better liars. Overly harsh punishments can end up backfiring and making better liars out of our children. Studies indicate that people who believe they've been treated unfairly will justify taking something back as retribution.[11] This tells us something about people who have been treated unjustly in our society, but it also points to the futility of authoritarian rules and punishments when dealing with kids; these harsh techniques actually create the conditions for worse behavior. Consider the young woman from chapter 2 who was stealing from her strict parents.

The most effective approach, therefore, is not to fear and shame the bad behavior but to draw out the best, honest behavior. Fairness, trust, and connection should take precedence over punishment. The most effective line, according to research, is to say, "I won't be mad if you took the cookie, and if you tell the truth, I'll be happy."[12] This works because kids want to make us happy.

This method of drawing out the best teaches our kids that the truth will make everyone—most importantly, us—happier. It will also make them happier. However, if we use this technique, we have to mean it and be happy if they admit to taking the cookie. This becomes especially important when they are teenagers and the stakes are higher. We want kids to feel comfortable telling the truth about sex and drugs and sneaking out at night so we can help them make the best decisions. We also need to let kids make their own mistakes—that's part of letting them grow up, and one of the hardest.

Ideally, we give our children a chance to tell the truth. In the long run, this should be more important than today's broken vase or tomorrow's mysteriously missing cookie. If we make it safe for our kids to be honest, vulnerable, and reflective without getting mired in shame, they'll develop the ability to admit that they're wrong. Part of teaching kids to reflect is helping them see the larger social costs of dishonesty. A friend of mine described being dragged back to a store as a teenager to apologize for shoplifting. The shop owner explained that the theft was not merely a matter of a fifty-cent candy bar; the clerk would also have to tell her boss that the candy bar was missing, and the accountant would have to include that missing merchandise in their accounting, and the clerks would mistrust their customers and colleagues, and so on. My friend explained that when she was able to see the web of cause and effect of her seemingly minor transgression, she felt compassion for the suffering she'd caused. That is what kept her from stealing again.

As we've seen, children will lie for different reasons as they age. At first, they lie to get what they want. This is perfectly rational, when you think about it—they are neurologically incapable of understanding long-term consequences. And they lie in self-interest because, let's face it, children are fairly self-centered in temperament and in how their brains are wired. They also lie to avoid punishment, even when we catch them with chocolate smeared all over their face and hands (when they get older, they'll at least know to wipe the chocolate off their face first). As they get even older, kids may lie for attention or social empowerment, which can get increasingly risky.[13] At this stage, instead of just punishing them for lying, we need to help them find better ways to get their social needs met.

reflection What did you lie about as a kid, and how did your parents respond? What do you do to cultivate a space in which your children feel safe enough to be honest with you?

The Truth about White Lies and Apologizing

How are we supposed to respond when our partner asks if an outfit makes them look fat? Do we force our child to tell Grandma how much they love that hideous plaid turtleneck they've just unwrapped for their birthday? Do we make them apologize on the playground, particularly when they don't mean it? These scenarios reveal that the issue of honesty is not always cut and dry. There are often social and relational aspects of truth telling to consider.

Well, kids can always thank Grandma for the gift and leave it at that, but I'm afraid I haven't yet figured out how best to respond to the "How does this dress make me look?" conundrum. Still, some considerations are worth digging into when it comes to those playground apologies.

Many of us who recall forced apologies growing up probably primarily remember that they usually just led to a smug smirk the instant the adjudicating adult turned their back. We all also know how the power of an authentic apology can be profound. But forced apologies can unwittingly teach kids that apologies are short-term "get out of jail free" cards. As parents, we need to look honestly at the efficacy of those artificial apologies. Who are we actually trying to make feel better—the other child, their parents, or ourselves? Sure, forcing your kid to apologize can be a handy social lubricant on the playground, but some other approaches are worth considering when you have the time.

More effective than apologies are *amends*. Amends (think about amendments to the Constitution) are not apologies per se, but fixes and improvements. I recently watched my friend Julia suggest that her older son check in with her younger boy to see if there was anything he could do to make it better after the big one had knocked over the smaller one while playing. The younger boy responded that he wanted a hug, and the older offender offered one. I remarked on the profundity of the moment, and Julia laughed, saying, "It doesn't usually go that smoothly, but that's what we're sort of aiming for."

When we jump on kids to apologize for a minor infraction, we may inadvertently drive them deeper into defensiveness, especially if their brains are already shut down from the stress of a conflict. Worse, if our children associate apologies with shame or punishment, they are unlikely to spontaneously apologize in the long run. This is why Jane Nelsen (author of *Positive Discipline*) recommends "connecting before correcting"—get down to the child's level and help them calm down if they just experienced conflict.[14] Doing this allows them to bring their insular and prefrontal cortices online, which enables them to take the other child's perspective and find a creative resolution to the conflict. From there, we might help kids reflect on how their behavior made the other child feel, encourage them to connect, and ask what they can do for the other child (if the other kid is willing)—whether this means an apology, a hug, or simply handing back the stolen toy. Kids who make things right in this way are found to act more altruistically down the road.[15,16]

One day, after we eventually get that dreaded phone call from school or from another angry parent about our kid's behavior, we can talk through or even role-play what an appropriate amends might be. Some useful questions (again from Jane Nelsen) include the following:

- What happened, and why?

- What were the results, and how did they affect you and others?

- What did you learn?

- How can you make it better?

Sometimes a consequence might still be in order, but if a child can make genuine amends, our validating and encouraging that prosocial behavior is far better than punishment for its own sake. If we create a space in which children feel safe, calm, and nondefensive, they'll be far more likely to make amends or apologize.

We can also model and practice apologizing and making amends for our children, as well as model receiving the same from others and practicing forgiveness. Another option is to share stories about times we've made mistakes and wish we could have behaved differently or made a heartfelt apology or amends. Relating with our children in this way not only changes the culture of our family but also nudges our larger communities toward problem solving, connection, and forgiveness—and away from a punitive culture of "zero tolerance" policies.

reflection What are your values around making amends or apologies? How do you model these for your kids? When was the last time you apologized or made amends to your partner or someone else in front of your children?

When we examine the science and wisdom of honesty, we find it may be more complicated than a matter of truth and lies. Honesty creates safety and freedom for everyone. While none of us will ever be perfect, we can all find more effective ways to teach the importance of truthfulness.

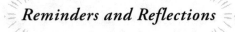

Reminders and Reflections

- Honesty *and* dishonesty are habits that can be made or broken.

- Honesty *and* dishonesty are contagious.

- When young kids lie, it's often due to a lack of brain development or a wish to not let you down, rather than a lack of morality or a manipulation.

- Speaking your truth can be an act of generosity to you and others.

- How do you create the conditions for honesty or dishonesty in yourself and your family?

- What factors make it more difficult to tell the truth to others?

- Starting when kids (and crimes) are small, reinforce telling the truth over punishing the lie.

- Consider ways to connect and correct to encourage authentic amends rather than forcing a fake apology.

CHAPTER 8

growing up with a
grit and growth mindset

(Raising Determination—Adhitthana)

The Buddha was born into a culture that believed in *samsara*—the never-ending cycle of death and rebirth. But following his enlightenment, he declared that it was possible to transcend the endless loop of birth, suffering, and death. In today's language, we could say that while most people at the time of Buddha held a *fixed* mindset, the Buddha (and other renowned spiritual leaders) displayed a *growth* mindset—believing in the unlimited potential of the human heart and mind.

Professor of psychology Carol Dweck is well known for her research on growth and fixed mindsets, both of which are largely a product of our upbringing.[1] People with growth mindsets believe they can improve through practice; in turn, they work harder, come up with more creative solutions, and ultimately thrive. When they encounter a setback, they don't blame anyone or anything else. They express a love of learning and seek out challenges for new learning opportunities; they see effort and determination as part of the learning process. These people are far less likely to give up when facing challenges, and they seek out feedback from others in order to improve. In contrast, those with a fixed mindset tend to believe they are incapable of becoming stronger, smarter, or better. They're also far more likely to blame others or themselves and give up, whether it's in school, sports, or relationships. A fixed mindset focuses on *looking* capable rather than *being* capable. People who think this way avoid challenges that threaten their self-image, seeking out easy and familiar success instead. They find feedback unhelpful or even threatening.

We can all do our part to shift to a growth mindset that keeps us from giving up. Angela Duckworth famously refers to this attitude as *grit*. In her words, grit is a combination of "perseverance and passion for long-term goals" that is associated with success, happiness, and resilience.[2] The best-known spiritual leaders—the Buddha, Jesus, Moses, and Muhammad—never gave up. They all had grit. They were each motivated by something within, as well as by the challenge and excitement of creating a unique path to helping others. Somewhere along the line, each of them tapped into *flow*, that state of effortless action mentioned in chapter 5. We too can cultivate this flow. In fact, I think most of us have felt that near-magical state of engagement at some point or another. It's the ultimate intrinsic motivation for the brain.

reflection   In what aspects of life do you have a growth or fixed mindset? What about in relation to your kids? What keeps you from giving up?

External Motivations

At least half of the parents I meet for therapy are concerned about their children's motivation. We need motivation and determination in almost everything we do in life—school, extracurricular activities, the spiritual path, parenting, you name it. So how can we motivate our families and ourselves? Unfortunately, we're a culture that seems habituated toward extrinsic motivation. Author Daniel Pink examines the science of motivation in his wonderful book *Drive*.[3] He notes that external motivators like rewards, punishments, bribes, threats, and promises may work in the short term but, over time, can backfire. Emphasizing rewards, for example, ultimately diminishes intrinsic motivation, creativity, and quality of work. By focusing on rewards over behaviors, we set the stage for shortcuts and even ethical lapses to earn the reward—think sleazy lawyers (or, okay, sleazy therapists) padding their hours. That's not to suggest that rewards inevitably *cause* sloppy work or sketchy ethics, but they do tend to cultivate the conditions under which such problems arise. We see this all the time in corporate boardrooms and children's classrooms.

As author Alfie Kohn points out in *Punished by Rewards*, "Rewards motivate students to get rewards."[4] Imagine that you pay your middle-school-aged kid ten dollars a book to get her to read. Is she more likely to choose *War and Peace* or to pick a pile of graphic novels that she can polish off in an afternoon? Not only will she be tempted to behave in the way that brings her the promised reward fastest, but she'll hardly develop a newfound love of literature. To make matters worse, constant rewards tend to escalate tolerance to those rewards, while also teaching kids killer negotiation skills. These skills may be great for the boardroom, but they are maddening for your living room. One desperate family I worked with had given so many rewards that their fifteen-year-old son, Sam, had become an expert negotiator. He basically held the family finances hostage. Sam would barely clear his plate from the dinner table without the promise of a music gift card loaded with an ever-higher spending limit (which, he confessed in therapy, he typically traded away for marijuana).

It isn't that we need to write off rewards altogether; we just need to pick and use them wisely. It turns out that occasional and unexpected rewards are actually more effective in cultivating *intrinsic* motivation and avoiding hostage situations, like the one in Sam's family. A surprise treat—say, an ice cream cone after completing a tough afternoon of chores—will be more likely to encourage motivation now *and* in the future. Think of it as shifting from an *if/then* to a *now/that* approach. But don't make these rewards too regular. "Great job on your homework, now let's go for ice cream" only works as long as it's not *too* frequent or predictable. In technical terms, this approach to reward is known as a *variable-rate reinforcement schedule*, and it's the most effective way to create a habit.

For most of us, this is common sense. If we offer our kid a treat to get them to finish writing their essay, will they do the *best* job or the *fastest* job? If we reward them for getting an A on that essay, we set the stage for them doing whatever it takes to get the promised reward, maybe even cutting a few corners in the process. If we want to instill grit and lasting motivation, however, we need to reward grit and motivation themselves (more on this point in a little bit) rather than the end result.

External rewards are also more likely to work when we acknowledge the unpleasantness of required tasks and explain their importance. It's helpful to let kids do jobs and chores in creative ways that make those tasks more fun or efficient—for example, "You're right—taking out the trash is boring and annoying, but we need a house that isn't stinky so friends will come over. And I love your creative idea of taking out the trash with your roller skates on!" If you are inclined to offer praise for doing good work, be as specific as possible—"I appreciate your doing the trash this morning without being reminded. The kitchen smells much better, and you even washed your hands afterward. High five to the guy with clean hands!" External rewards like money will buy you a powerful, quick response, but getting down to your kid's level, making eye contact, and giving specific praise in the form of attention and affection will bring longer-lasting results, even if it has somewhat less of an immediate punch. These relational rewards don't diminish the way material rewards do. And sure, by the time your kids are tweens, they may roll their eyes, but that praise and affection will still fire up their brain's reward circuits beneath that too-cool exterior. Finally, consider what you're conditioning in the long run. Would you rather have your kids motivated in life by authentic, compassionate connection or by cold, hard cash?

Speaking of cash, many of us grew up having to do household chores linked to some kind of allowance—essentially, money in exchange for work. However, newer research suggests that linking allowance to chores can have the unintended side effects we see when we predictably reward a behavior—namely, contract renegotiation under the threat of labor strikes (though maybe we do want to encourage that skill in the long run). Many experts now recommend separating *family chores* from *extra chores*. The former are jobs we are simply expected to do around the house (which builds work ethic and family connection); the latter are additional things we can do to learn the value of hard work, earning, and saving.[5]

reflection   What external rewards systems do you use with your children? How effective have they been over time? What "now/that" surprises can you use with your kids in the place of predictable "if/then" rewards?

Intrinsic Motivators

What inspired you as a child? What truly motivates you today? I'd bet the answers have less to do with money and more to do with feeling a sense of meaning, helping others, creating, and enjoying autonomy. If it's not about rewards and punishments, pleasure and pain, desire and aversion, then it must be something more meaningful, and that's just it. Meaning, helping, and autonomy are the keys to motivation in everything from management theories to Montessori. Consider great leaders or spiritual figures, whether Eastern or Western—they creatively blazed a new path and were motivated by helping others. We all share these lasting, deep-seated motivations, and they are the same motivations we want to arouse and encourage in our kids.

After I published my first book, I calculated what I was paid for all the work I put into it; it came out to less than forty cents an hour. Clearly, money wasn't my primary motivation. But I loved almost every forty-cent hour of writing, to the point that each round of edits felt not like a chore but a challenge. For me, writing taps into *flow*—that psychological state of absorption that comes about when the satisfaction of the challenge *is* the reward. With survival needs met and exceeded, most of us seek out the dopamine hit that accompanies flow as much or more than we seek out money.

We need intrinsic rewards. They feel good and encourage us to keep going through inevitable challenges. Unfortunately, their absence makes us fundamentally unhappy and more likely to give up when the going gets hard. One reason extrinsic rewards don't work as well is that they ultimately diminish our sense of autonomy. Is it any wonder, then, that independence-oriented teenagers don't respond well to sticker charts, while younger kids appreciate them? Autonomy doesn't mean *complete* freedom of choice. Let's be realistic—if we gave kids total freedom, they'd likely spend their days playing games on their devices and living on a steady diet of junk food. What autonomy really means is a range of choices within given limits that involve accountability and connection to others.

To encourage a sense of autonomy and meaning, we want our kids to become *engaged*, not merely *compliant*. This is why making chores into a game works. It is also why we want to encourage our kids' feelings of competence and mastery by helping them connect what they learn in useful ways. Practicing their Spanish when they see signs around town *en Español*, applying math to their lemonade-stand business, using science to explain the weather, and planning the processes for growing, preparing, and cooking their food are fun, effective motivators. They all offer a sense of mastery and ownership in what kids can do in their daily lives.

But it's up to us adults to nurture these intrinsic motivations. The research is clear—intrinsically motivated people perform better, feel happier, live healthier, enjoy higher self-esteem, and have more stable relationships than those trained with external rewards.[6] Of course, we live in the real world where schoolwork and chores are often unmeaningful, and we can't stop for a teachable moment in an attempt to creatively encourage intrinsic motivation every time someone has to take out the "stupid garbage." So, again, give yourself and your kids a break—do your best and strive for a middle path.

reflection   In what ways can you use creativity, meaning, and connection to motivate your family?

Praise Smarter, Not Harder

I was born in 1977, on the cusp of the "participation trophy" generation. When I was a kid, much of parenting research focused on self-esteem: High self-esteem was credited with success in life, love, school, and work. Low self-esteem was the culprit behind academic issues, violence, drug use, promiscuity, and more. However, a few decades of emphasizing self-esteem resulted in little more than kids who were *more* vulnerable than those of the generation before. Studies even indicated that bullies often had high self-esteem; they merely acted out in order to maintain their self-esteem and status. Not all kids with high self-esteem become bullies, but researchers began noticing links between self-esteem-focused parenting and later emotional fragility and narcissism in kids.[7]

Social scientists have discovered ways to encourage self-esteem without the accompanying narcissism, while at the same time promoting grit, determination, and growth. The crucial difference comes in praising *effort* (something kids can control) rather than *outcome* (which they often cannot). Think back to growth and fixed mindsets—notice any similarities?

I enjoyed an early childhood of tremendous success at almost everything I tried, and I regularly heard how smart and wonderful I was. However, things began to shift around fifth grade. I discovered that I was *not* the best at everything. As a result, if I wasn't the best at a particular activity, I began quitting. At first, it was soccer. I wasn't the star, so I quit. Music came next. I was decent at playing guitar but not great, so I stopped going to lessons. Before long, I became uninterested in anything that took long-term commitment and hard work. When I didn't receive the merit badges that the other sixth graders were earning in Boy Scouts, I burst into tears. My scoutmaster gently explained to me that merit badges require *work*—you don't get them merely for showing up. It sounds absurd in retrospect, but I was devastated. By ninth grade, I stopped doing homework and barely showed up for class; my primary extracurricular activity was smoking pot behind the school—but I'll save that story for another book.

Around this time, my parents got some useful advice about parenting and determination from our family therapist: "the number one rule of parenting is to *never give up*." And so my devoted parents did what the experts suggested: they praised my talents and focused on my self-esteem—an approach that 85 percent of American parents agree with, and why not?[8] Unfortunately, this way of "never giving up" completely backfired, leaving kids like me underprepared for the pains of adulthood. Just because my mom thought I was handsome, my dad thought I was smart, and my therapist thought I was brave didn't mean the rest of the world agreed.

As it turns out, overpraise leads kids to feeling out of control, fragile, and risk-averse, in addition to all the other stereotypical qualities we've heard about the so-called millennials. It's the overpraised kids who suffer from learned helplessness, quit activities left and right, maintain their self-esteem by putting others down, exaggerate their achievements, and cheat.

The best way to encourage resilience and determination is not through praising "natural talent" or "intelligence" (which are fixed mindset views) but by reinforcing and rewarding the effort and determination behind success—the growth mindset. In one study, Carol Dweck examined the effect of different kinds of praise on hundreds of fifth graders.[9] Students were given a simple puzzle and were then scored and praised when they completed it. The difference between the two random groups in the study was the type of praise they received—half were praised for being smart; the other half, for their hard work or effort. After round one, the kids in each group were offered the choice of either a harder puzzle or an easier one. Most of those praised for their smarts went with the easier option, but the kids praised for their effort challenged themselves with the harder test. In round three of the study, all the kids received a nearly impossible puzzle to solve. The "effort" group worked harder and longer, seemingly relishing the challenge. However, the "smart" group gave up almost immediately. By the fourth round, all the kids got a break with an easy puzzle. Not surprisingly, the "effort" kids raised their performance level by about 30 percent, whereas the "smart" kids decreased by 20 percent. Similar studies show the same results.

Why does receiving praise for being intelligent lead to low frustration tolerance, giving up, and cheating? The answer appears to be that although we can largely control effort, our culture has taught us that intelligence and talent are static qualities. If kids believe their intelligence level is innate, they tend to dismiss the importance of effort. Still other studies have found that if we teach kids that intelligence can be strengthened through hard work, they work harder and perform better.[10]

reflection   What kind of praise did you receive growing up? How do you praise your own children? How can you shift toward praising effort over outcome in your family?

Despite inadvertently breeding determination out of American kids, young kids don't naturally give up as they approach a challenging goal. I spent a recent summer watching my one-year-old learn to walk. He never gave up. He teetered, he tottered, he tumbled, and he fell, but he got right back up and tried again. And it felt natural for me to praise his effort and encourage him to keep going. The real challenge will be my keeping up the praise on effort over outcome as he grows up. I can hear your responses already: "We're praising our kids wrong, too? Now I can't tell them they are smart?" No and no, and nor am I suggesting that we all start telling our kids they are lazy and dumb. There's not a right or wrong; as with everything, there's a middle path of praise. All I'm saying is we might want to shift the balance. (Of course, I think my own son is perfect and a genius and want to tell him that and often do.)

Shifting the emphasis to praising effort may feel strange if we grew up praising (or being praised for) smarts and self-esteem. Even as a therapist, I reflexively want to praise my clients just for showing up, but that's not always the most helpful thing to do. On better days I can take a wiser, longer view to prepare kids for a world beyond the palace gates, where not everyone else will see them as quite so magical.

Praising differently doesn't mean applying more effort. My friend, psychologist Mitch Abblett, suggests shifting from *praising* (which is general) to *prizing* (which is more specific). What's more, our praise must be authentic or it will backfire. Once they are about seven, kids can tell when adults are being disingenuous with their praise. By the time they are teenagers, kids can tell which of their peers are struggling, because those are the kids getting the most self-esteem praise.[11] Similarly, kids can pick out the high-achieving kids, because they see them get the toughest, most-specific feedback.

Essentially, we need to channel my old colleague and praise smarter, not harder. Praise kids for staying on task and not getting distracted. Praise them for hard work. And praise the finer points of their effort—not just for winning the game, but also for seeing the opportunities to pass or shoot. Talk about what worked and what didn't, and review their best work to remind them of their own potential. Angela Duckworth suggests stressing the importance of a positive mindset and aspects of identity—for example, by saying, "Great job! Our family doesn't quit until the end!"

Moreover, we want to strike a balance between too much praise and too little. Robert Cloninger, a psychiatrist and geneticist at Washington University in St. Louis, found that intermittent reinforcement and praise (like the "now/that" surprise ice cream) lead to kids giving more effort in the long run.[12] Too much praise and kids don't make the effort after the rewards fade; too little praise and kids don't have enough incentive to try. In his study, Cloninger used an MRI to examine the brains of children, especially their orbital and medial prefrontal cortices, which monitor the reward system. With the optimal balance of reinforcement, these areas tell the rest of our brains, "Don't quit—the reward is coming!" In this way, we become hooked on the positive feeling of praise associated with a rise in the reward chemical *dopa*.

reflection Recall a time in your life when you discovered that you could do more than you expected. How did you do it? Now remember a time when you saw your children do more than you thought they could? What factors were involved?

Little Disciplines Lead to Larger Ones

Social psychologist Roy Baumeister, an early critic of the self-esteem movement, found that determination and willpower increase when activated and practiced.[13] He also observed the phenomena of ego depletion that I first mentioned in chapter 2. Ego depletion strikes when we're tired, are in an unfamiliar setting, or have low glucose—a necessary fuel for our prefrontal cortex. Sleeping fewer than six hours leads to ego depletion, which is also correlated with overeating (and obesity), as well as drops in willpower and even IQ. These findings stress the link between self-care and our ability to be focused and disciplined.

Discipline is not some magical trait that some people are born with and some aren't. We can actually increase our willpower with self-care and by exercising the muscle of discipline. Practicing discipline in small ways (e.g., using our nondominant hand or saying "yes" instead of "yeah") correlates with persistence in other realms. The positive value of practicing discipline makes a good argument for the value of chores. Unfortunately, chores are on the decline in U.S. households—a recent study found that only 28 percent of parents assign chores, despite 82 percent of them growing up having to do chores themselves.[14] Yet, according to research, starting kids with small chores when they are three or four is the best predictor of success (in academics, employment, and relationships) in young adulthood.[15] Other studies have found chores to be a later predictor of mental health.[16] Maybe making the bed every morning is actually as important as your grandmother suggested.

I recommend *family chores*—they're a lot more fun, and they teach the important skill of working together. Besides, cleaning up leads to a lot more benefits than just a tidy space to live in. Research shows that a messy work environment results in more distraction, less compassion, difficulty delaying gratification, and decreased ability to make healthy choices.[17] Perhaps this is why so many spiritual traditions emphasize small daily disciplines of ritual, diet, prayer or meditation, and clean monastic cells.

Cultivating Grit but Knowing When to Quit

While sticking it out is important, so too is having the wisdom to know when to let go and use our energy more wisely. A popular meditation instruction given to beginners is to keep sitting until you can't stand it and then sit for one minute more. We all have to know when it's okay to quit, but that time shouldn't be in our darkest hour. When we quit at a low, we hardwire a negative memory, which can lead to avoidance and even phobia in the future. This is why when a kid falls off a bike while learning to ride, it's best to encourage them to get back on the bike and ride home (with us right there next to them). Once they've gained more confidence, they can decide if they want to keep going. The same holds true with other experiences and activities—don't let the fall or failure be what sticks in your (or their) memory. If violin lessons are a disaster, wait until after the concert to stop, and don't quit those karate or Brazilian jiu-jitsu lessons until after the next belt test.

One nine-year-old in my practice was frustrated with her softball team. "Sophie wants to quit," her mother explained. "Should I let her? She doesn't like it, but she's afraid of hurting her team's feelings." The question of whether to let our kids quit comes down to intention—yet it can also be an agonizing choice. After the mother and I discussed the pros and cons, she ultimately decided to let her daughter quit at the end of the season, thereby allowing the girl to feel proud of having stuck it out and fulfilling her commitment to her teammates. Sophie didn't feel proud of all of her strikeouts and missed catches, but she did feel pride at sticking it out—the most important lesson of any commitment.[18] Commitments teach determination, and study after study shows that when people commit in front of others, they are more likely to follow through with their stated goals. When your children begin a new activity or project, be sure to discuss their commitment to the project at the outset.

Colleges and employers want those kids who show commitment early in life. College admissions officers can see through overstuffed résumés, but two years of extracurriculars in high school seems to be a magic number—there is a real correlation with college graduation rates, and it is a predictor of generosity.[19] I recently heard from an Ivy

League admissions officer that colleges are considering limiting space on applications for only two extracurricular commitments in order to encourage greater depth.

reflection How do you decide when to quit or keep going? What are your family's values around knowing when to quit? At what points in your life have you quit and regretted it? What about a time that you quit and it was the right choice? In retrospect, how did you know?

Setting and Achieving Goals

Specific, realistic, step-by-step goals are vital to sticking things out, especially for kids. Carol Dweck differentiates between performance goals (with external measurements like grades and scores) and learning goals (with internal assessments like personal satisfaction). Striking the right balance between these two is crucial for your children. What's more, committing to an activity over time (whether it's running or making a sculpture) builds patience and stamina. So give your kids opportunities for longer projects. Weekend role-playing camps, intricate board games, and, yes, even some video games can be extended activities with multiple steps that will help your kids build determination and executive functions.[20]

With their brains not fully developed, kids will struggle to make the link between homework and goals down the road. Smaller goals with smaller rewards along the way will help them experience the reinforcing power of success *as* the reward. At the same time, you can maintain high expectations and high levels of support, reminding your children, "Climbing this mountain is going to be hard, but I know you can do it. It will feel great at the top." Praising their progress and strategic thinking is also useful, even when they fail. When they do fail, it's good to remind them that failure is part of the process—learning from mistakes is a big part of future success.

For academically "underachieving" kids, I encourage parents not to set specific grades as goals, which can lead to unwanted side effects. Rather, I stress goals that indicate efforts that lead to success—sitting at the front of the classroom, asking questions in class every day, and requesting extra help after school. What struggling kids need is not an A at any cost, but the confidence to ask questions when they don't understand and a trusting, mutually respectful relationship with adults.

Healthy self-talk also motivates us to meet our goals. As adults, we often use mental narrators to walk us through the steps of a challenging project—changing those first diapers, for example. For kids who struggle with ADHD and other executive function difficulties, teaching this type of self-narration can prove particularly beneficial. The most effective form of self-talk, according to research, is in the second and third person. Rather than the *Little Engine That Could* ("I think I can, I think I can"), research indicates it's most effective to cheer yourself on with your own name ("Chris, I know you can, I know you can").[21]

In addition, if you truly want your kids to learn to stick things out through challenges, let them create goals that align with their passions. Most "successful" people in all walks of life will tell you that following their bliss got them where they are. Countless studies find that if you truly like your job or college major, you are more likely to stick with it and improve. Encourage your kids to study what they love, and their careers will often follow. This may also be easier than switching careers later. Even so, many of my happiest friends went from being lawyers to screenwriters, or worked as nurses before becoming artists, or transitioned from corporate consultants to spiritual counselors—these are all people who jumped around between careers before returning to their original, deeply held passions—or, like me, combined the impractical and creative (writing) with a day job as a clinician. If your children work at what they love, they will be far more likely to find a way.

Finally, do what you can to alleviate stress. Stress erodes motivation over time, and it has a negative effect on learning and health, both physical and mental. Stress disrupts the development of executive function, emotional regulation, creativity, and other important "noncognitive" skills. We see this over and over again in studies on adverse childhood experiences—abuse, neglect, even inconsistent parenting. Each adverse experience stacks up to create unhealthy, unhappy adults. Secure attachment through calm, consistent interaction leads to positive brain development, allowing kids the safety to process the world with clarity and determination. In the end, children need this in order to set and meet healthy goals in life.

As parents, no matter what happens, just keep going. Remember that family therapist's number one rule—*never give up*. We never give up on our kids, and that's the best lesson they could ever receive about determination. Like many things in life, parenthood never has an end goal in mind—there's no final destination. It's a journey for all of us, which means we keep going through pregnancy or the adoption process, we keep going through the diapers and sleeplessness and food throwing, we keep going through toothaches and tantrums, we keep going through bullying and mean girls, and we keep going through all the heartbreak and challenges of adolescence and adulthood. And we never give up.

Reminders and Reflections

- External material rewards and punishments
  tend to work only in the short term.

- Intrinsic rewards such as meaning, connection, and
  creativity are more effective in the long term.

- Shift the balance toward "now/that," rather
  than "if/then," rewards.

- In what ways can you praise effort over outcome in your family?

- What are your family's values around knowing when to quit?

- Encourage a growth mindset in your kids and teach them
  that skill and intelligence can be cultivated through work.

- Praise and model resilience in the face of mistakes and setbacks.

- Consider small chores and daily rituals as a bridge
  that leads to larger acts of self-discipline.

CHAPTER 9

the kindness contagion

(Raising Lovingkindness—Metta)

Your life is going to be a gradual process of becoming kinder
and more loving: Hurry up. Speed it along. Start right now.
AUTHOR GEORGE SAUNDERS[1]

Two things can happen when we start a family. We can feel the deep connection and compassion for other parents across the world, or we can become tribal, fearful, and protective. Usually, it's a combination of both. I still remember the incredible love I felt not just toward my son after he was born, but also toward everyone we encountered those first few weeks. Maybe it was the oxytocin flowing, but colors seemed brighter and birds sang more beautifully as I wandered about the world grinning dopily at strangers. But then, one afternoon, when a car didn't stop at a crosswalk to let us pass, I experienced a blast of self-righteous indignation toward the driver that I'd never before experienced.

The same summer Leo was born, a new war ravaged yet another distant part of the world. The anguish on the faces of the parents as they searched rubble for their missing children was more immediate and acute to me than ever before. It occurred to me that those who were dropping bombs on cities surely felt that *they* were doing what they *had to do* to keep their own children safe. Becoming a parent helped me realize that underneath all of our differences, all creatures want more than anything to keep their families safe from harm. But how quickly the warmth and compassion we have for our children switches to fear and hatred of the *other*! And that's what oxytocin is all about—at the same time that it's associated with feelings of love and connection, it also relates to our experiences of jealousy, protection, and possessiveness—that "mama bear" or "papa bear" response. If there are indeed two sides of love, this chapter is about fostering the bright, hopeful, positive side through deliberate practices of lovingkindness (as opposed to loving*fear* or loving*anger*), knowing that fear, anger, and hatred will never be defeated with more of the same.

When we meet suffering, we're all hardwired for a fight-or-flight response (which includes freezing and "forget it" reactions). Over time, these can lead to anger, avoidance, anxiety, or depression. Although these strong emotions can energize us into action, they just as often lead to our turning away from the suffering we meet in the world. When our greatest spiritual leaders first encountered suffering, however, it sparked a compassionate drive in them to free themselves and all others. No matter our conditioning, we can all turn toward suffering through the practices of mindfulness and compassion in a process that psychologist Shelley Taylor calls "tending and befriending," rather than turning away.[2]

According to some Buddhist teachings, lovingkindness refers to the wish for all sentient beings—including our children's other caregivers—and the natural world around them to experience happiness, whereas compassion refers to the desire that all other creatures be free from suffering. Like every tradition's variation on the Golden Rule, compassion essentially means treating others—strangers and friends—how we want them to treat us. Although I won't always make such a clear distinction in this chapter, the important point I want to convey is that whether we call it lovingkindness or compassion, they are qualities that Eastern philosophy and Western science agree we can cultivate in ourselves and our children with practice. They also agree that compassion training makes us happier, healthier, more productive, and—not surprisingly—more popular. Compassion-trained toddlers are more apt to share their stickers, be more flexible, delay gratification, and exhibit stronger scores on measures of executive functions.[3]

Some Eastern traditions teach that this change begins with ourselves. Putting ourselves first may feel a little strange to many of us. However, caring for yourself *is* caring for your child, because it all starts with us. This is where self-compassion enters the picture, especially for parents.

We all make mistakes. We all fall short of being the parent we thought we would or should be. There are moments when I hate myself after losing my cool, and I regularly reserve my most creative insults for myself when I forget to pack Leo's snack or monkey. Unfortunately, self-hatred isn't known for its ability to overcome self-hatred, which is why self-compassion is so powerful. Forgiveness begins with ourselves. Self-forgiveness and self-compassion do not make us weak or selfish, nor do they indicate that we have lowered our standards. In fact, research repeatedly indicates that they make us more resilient in the face of challenges, more willing to compromise and apologize, and more compassionate toward others.[4] Even when we hold dark secrets and nearly unbearable regrets, we can still learn to practice lovingkindness, compassion, and forgiveness for ourselves.

reflection How has becoming a parent changed your attitude toward others in terms of compassion? Where has compassion come to you more naturally? In what ways have you encountered more limits to your compassion? What does self-compassion mean to you?

Here's a practice that addresses some of the points above. I adapted it from ideas by Chris Germer, Kristen Neff, and Susan Bögels.[4,5]

PRACTICE Self-Compassion

Take a moment to sit comfortably and allow your eyes to close. Bring to mind a difficult situation in your parenting over the past few weeks—not too big,

just something relatively small. What is the scene?
Who was there? What were they saying or doing?
Take a moment for the image to become clear. Then
bring your awareness to all the sensations, emotions,
thoughts, and judgments that come to you right now
in the moment.

Take a few breaths. Then place a hand on your heart,
cheek, or arm. Using your own name, say to yourself,
"This is hard. This is a moment of suffering. I work to
be a good parent, and I may not be perfect, but I am
a good-enough parent." Use whatever words work for
you. Take a few more moments to breathe and feel
the sensations, noticing any shift in your physical or
emotional experience.

Finally, remind yourself in some way that all
parents struggle. We all fall short of who we wish
to be. We all make mistakes. That's what makes us
human, and that's what connects us as parents. We all
struggle and suffer in similar ways.

Take a few more breaths as you reflect on this.
Then allow your eyes to open.

Personally, practicing self-compassion has helped me develop more compassion not just for myself but for others as well, including my own kids
and parents. (As one particularly wise teen I see in my practice recently
remarked, "My parents get the angriest with me when I make the
same mistakes they did at my age.") Having compassion for my own
mistakes as a parent has helped me have more compassion for my
own parents. As the old joke goes, "I used to be the best parent in the
world until I had my own kids." Becoming more compassionate for
ourselves also builds resilience, equanimity, and determination—all
qualities we want to foster in our children. How better to do this
than to embody them ourselves?

reflection   What are some ways you can practice and model self-care and self-compassion in your life? In what ways do you encourage self-compassion in your family?

The Research

To begin with, we are all born with the seeds—neurons and DNA—of lovingkindness and compassion. Babies become more upset when they hear other babies crying than when they hear a recording of their own cries; they soothe upset kids with a gentle touch or other offerings (a toy or bottle); and they even spontaneously help adults who appear to be struggling.[6]

Research also shows that empathy and compassion are good for us. Even the Dalai Lama, the embodiment of compassion, says that although compassion is great for the people we give it to, we ourselves are its primary beneficiaries. Kids who share in kindergarten are more likely to graduate high school and hold full-time jobs; those who don't are more likely to struggle with mental health and other issues.[7] Research also indicates that we get more happiness from cooperating than from competing. Kindness online pays off with more likes and compliments of others, leading to more social and business opportunities.[8] Barbara Fredrickson, a researcher at the University of North Carolina, has found that just seven weeks of lovingkindness practice increases love, joy, contentment, gratitude, pride, hope, curiosity, and a sense of wonder.[9] Lovingkindness practices also appear to help chronic pain, migraines, and symptoms of depression and PTSD.[10,11,12] Practicing lovingkindness makes us more emotionally intelligent and empathic, with those feelings leading to concrete compassionate actions, such as generosity.[13]

Research also illustrates that using a soft voice and gentle touch with ourselves or others turns on empathy and connection—the "attend and befriend" response—which shuts off "fight or flight." More friendships lead to better physical and mental health and even a longer life. Just holding a friend's hand in times of trouble deactivates the brain's fear response.[14] We naturally give this type of gentle touch to our children, but we should remember its importance in helping our partners and friends, including ourselves. Holding hands—even with a stranger—quiets the pain response, as does the simple act of looking at a picture of a loved one. Showing affection, like hugs and kisses after a boo-boo, really does make us feel better, and giving a gentle hug or pat on the back can calm the nervous system.[15]

Richie Davidson and his colleagues at the University of Wisconsin spent years studying contemplative practices, including compassion and lovingkindness meditations. They found that meditators who viewed images of suffering had heightened activity in regions of the brain related to connection, caring, and nurturing. The nonmeditators in the study displayed more stimulation in regions associated with unpleasant emotions that led to avoidance and turning away from the pain.[16] The group that practiced compassion meditation not only tolerated the viewed suffering better but also actively turned toward it with an apparent desire to alleviate what they saw. But even the nonmeditators in the study could be trained, in about a week, to increase activity in empathy-related parts of the brain. (It's also been shown that merely practicing mindfulness will increase compassionate and altruistic behavior.[17]) Davidson also found that meditation appeared to lead to greater neuroplasticity—that is, the ability to change our brain structure. It also positively affects parts of the brain related to immune functioning and other important operations of the body.[18]

Cultivating Kindness

Sadly, empathy in our children has been on the decline since 1979.[19] Today, 80 percent of middle schoolers report that their parents teach them that personal achievement is more important than caring for others.[20] What's happening here? Why is our culture facing a crisis of compassion?

Before we look at building compassion, let's consider the conditions that hinder compassion and kindness. As discussed earlier in this book, too much screen time can cut down on social skills, emotional intelligence, and empathy. At worst, we make insensitive or cruel comments online that we'd never say in person. Anonymity breeds threats and bullying, and we know that kids tend to bully when they are afraid of losing status. Bullying also increases when witnesses don't speak up out of fear. (The good news is that this "bystander effect" can be reduced through lovingkindness training.[21]) At a heightened level, cruelty flourishes when authority figures give explicit or tacit permission for emotional or physical violence, a phenomenon dubbed the "Lucifer Effect" by Phil Zimbardo, of Stanford prison experiment fame.[22]

Another kindness killer is stress. Sylvia Boorstein, a meditation teacher who wrote a wonderful book on the paramis, tells a story that captures this idea. Once, while she was teaching her grandson's first-grade class about mindfulness, a student asked her how she knew when she wasn't paying attention. Boorstein paused, reflected, and eventually responded, "I know I'm not paying attention if I am not feeling kind."[23] We can easily see this when our attitude toward others, especially our kids and partner, changes after fighting traffic following a stressful day at the office.

When we take care of ourselves, compassion comes easy. But studies have found that the more stressed we are, the less helpful we become. This even applies to seminary students and other professed do-gooders,[24] and I see this all the time with burned-out therapists; "compassion fatigue" is a risk for any caregiver. At the cellular level, oxytocin (the love hormone) and cortisol (the stress hormone) work on the very same receptors, making it almost impossible to feel both stressed and loving at the same time. Stress lights up the limbic system, which means that the outer cortices of our brain—the area associated with the ability to take someone else's perspective, control our impulses, and experience empathy—are shut down. It's no surprise that so much relational violence and bullying happens in high-stress, pressure-cooker schools.

reflection How does your level of compassion change in relation to stress or other factors in your life? How might being aware of this change help you in terms of your self-care?

When we are stressed, we forget the power of simple actions, such as lowering our bodies to our child's level, making eye contact, smiling, telling our child we love them, or holding a hug until our child lets go. But challenging times are precisely when we most need to practice the actions to foster connection. When our kids sense stress in our bodies or speech, they often react or pre-act, unwittingly setting negative patterns in motion.

The Power of Communication

We teach kindness by sharing it, offering our children the experience of empathy as we extend lovingkindness toward them and others. Compassion is also one of those social contagions, like generosity, that spreads from person to person.[25] Of course, it's often easier to have compassion for strangers in a distant country than those closer by. So consider what words and tone you use to describe your boss, in-laws, ex, and even the insensitive stranger who just cut you off on the highway. When we talk about "poor people," for example, it suggests that poverty is part of a person's identity, rather than their experience. When we regularly refer to "good guys" and "bad guys" in stories—not to mention in our social circle—how does that affect our kids' compassion and ability to see these people as people? This even holds true when discussing a bully or a bully's family—it's certain that they, too, are suffering in some tangible way. Keep in mind that someone, someday, will likely view *your* kid as the bully. Indeed, plenty of people who knew me when I was young would be surprised to hear me preaching the virtues of compassion.

It can take a while to realize that everyone deserves compassion. When I was a kid in 1981 and heard that Ronald Reagan had been shot, I ran to my parents and beamed, "Did you hear the good news? Someone finally shot Ronald Reagan!" After all, I had grown up hearing them complain endlessly about the new president. My mom crouched down and looked me in the eyes, saying, "Oh, Sweetie, even though we really disagree with him, we're never happy if someone gets hurt." That blew my four-year-old mind, and the memory stands out as a significant moment in my childhood. A few years later, at a time when I still believed that only "bad guys" went to jail, my mind and heart were blown open when our church did a clothing drive for people in prison. Here was a completely different perspective—people in prison were, well, *people*. How had I learned otherwise? It was partially from our punitive, "zero tolerance" culture, which makes teaching compassion and kindness truly an act of rebellion.

reflection   Who are the people in your life you struggle to hold in compassion? What about in your own family? What makes it difficult for you to feel compassion for them?

The way we speak can be more skillful, empathic, and accurate. It can be easy for adults and children to fall into "you're mean" or "he was selfish," rather than "he was acting selfish" or "*I'm* feeling hurt by your words." Ideally, we use "I" statements and employ words to describe *behavior* (rather than the *person*) when we speak with our children, especially when talking about others. More deeply, we can seek to understand a person's behavior rather than just label it. Every behavior communicates something that child doesn't have words or skills for. Rather than saying, "He's mean," we can ask what might be behind the other child's unkind behavior—for example, "Do you think he could be lonely or tired?" I know a couple who encourages their son to think of three reasons someone might have acted the way they did (like "Maybe he had a bad morning" or "I think he might have been jealous"—but the reason can't simply be, "Because he's mean").

Paradoxically, if you want to reinforce kindness and compassion, praise your child's character. Phrases like, "You are a kind and helpful person," are actually more effective than, "That was helpful to take the garbage out," though both are obviously welcome. Much like reinforcing hard work, making it about character reinforces their identity of being a helpful person. On the flip side, if your kid acts selfishly or unkindly, name the *behavior* as unkind, rather than suggesting he or she is inherently that way—for example, "You are a kind person. I'm surprised you did something unkind by grabbing his toy!" This reminds them and inspires them to be their best self, rather than shaming them out of being their worst self.

reflection   Bring to mind a recent situation in which someone in your family acted in a hurtful way. Think of three reasons they might have acted that way. What about a stranger?

Just Like Me . . .

Recognizing the commonalities we share with others enables us to activate our compassion and lovingkindness. Mirabai Bush says,

> Realizing that the other person is also just like me is the basis on which you can develop compassion, not only towards those around you but also towards your enemy. Normally, when we think about our enemy, we think about harming him. Instead, try to remember that the enemy is also a human being, just like me.[26]

As we get to know others, even just through spending time with them, we appreciate them more deeply. To paraphrase Thich Nhat Hanh, love *is* understanding, and understanding is love's other name.[27] Kids understand this, too. I once had a conversation with a fifteen-year-old who pondered whether truly understanding someone means you have to love them or if loving them means truly understanding them. Social psychologists might refer to something similar: the "proximity effect," or the fact that spending time with different kinds of people has been shown to break down bias.

We can practice recognizing our commonalities in various exercises. Ram Dass uses one called "Just Like Me" that highlights our similarities, especially our common joys and struggles with another person, and deemphasizes our differences. For children, get-to-know-you games like "The Wind Blows" and other icebreakers can build empathy, compassion, and kindness. Similar to the empathy-building activity mentioned earlier, you can encourage your kids to notice three commonalities with different people (especially difficult people) or even fictional characters. You can also encourage them to deliberately notice the helpful people in the world, as Mr. Rogers recommended.

When a group of eighteen-month-olds was asked to identify the emotions of characters in their picture books, they became more likely to share, help, and show concern for others.[28] Likewise, reading or writing first-person accounts of suffering has been shown to increase empathy.[29]

. . . And Yet Different—Examining Privilege

Part of cultivating kindness is seeing our similarities, but another part is learning about, respecting, and appreciating our differences. Bigotry emerges from fear, and—as Yoda famously pointed out—fear leads to anger, hatred, and suffering. The Buddha originally developed lovingkindness practices to conquer fear and its physiological manifestation in fight or flight. More recently, mindfulness has been shown to reduce racial bias.[30]

Exposing kids to different languages and stories that feature characters who look or act differently from us has been shown to boost empathy and respect. Traveling to other countries and trying different foods can help break down stereotypes when done thoughtfully. But you don't have to travel the world to find different cultures, of course—just take public transportation out of your own neighborhood or seek out restaurants, grocery stores, music, and languages different from your own. Recall that Siddhartha wasn't moved to universal compassion until he left his own gated community.

Our own culture, identity, and privilege are so natural to us that they might as well be invisible, just like water has become undetectable to a fish. We can discuss privilege skillfully with our children by discussing things or freedoms they have that others don't. The intention is to build awareness and inspire action, not generate shame or defensiveness. Reminding them about starving children across the globe (or across town) in the middle of a broccoli battle is unlikely to open hearts. Nagging your kids that they *should* feel grateful is more likely to result in shame and defensiveness. As emphasized in chapter 5, look for moments when your children are particularly open and receptive to discussing important topics. And remember, looking at privilege is a challenge, even for adults.

Privilege is simply the unearned advantages many of us live with by virtue of our social class, skin color, gender presentation, or any of the other identity markers in our culture. It's not too hard for most of us to see the ways in which others are disadvantaged, but it requires honesty, effort, and determination to accept that some of us live with systemic advantages or disadvantages that we neither earned nor asked for. Privilege is not something to be ashamed of, and we don't explore it only to be paralyzed with guilt. Rather, we explore our privilege so we can activate our empathy, compassion, and kindness to ally with others in the interest of justice. In this way, privilege becomes an asset, rather than a hindrance. The Buddha himself was born into significant privilege of his time—a wealthy, educated, powerful family. He renounced his wealth but lent his status to help liberate others. Similarly, we can strive to use our privilege to educate others (including our families and friends) to dismantle the unjust system.

reflection How are your children learning about privilege? What privileges do you and your family enjoy that can be used to help others? Which would you give up or lend if they could help others? What has been your journey in coming to understand aspects of your own privilege?

If you're having a little difficulty with this reflection, I highly recommend Peggy McIntosh's "White Privilege Checklist"[31] for those of you who, like me, fit that bill. Her work helped me uncover my own parental privileges as an educated, wealthy, white cisgendered man married to a woman in light of stories I've heard from friends, patients, and colleagues. My list isn't comprehensive (I'm sure I could include another page or two), but I encourage you to look it over and see which of my privileges might apply to you.

1. My child's textbooks acknowledge both the hardships and contributions of people of their background and identity.

2. My child can access education that accommodates their learning needs.

3. I can take my child to get their hair cut and feel confident the stylist will know how to cut their hair.

4. My child can take their electronics project to school and not be arrested or called a terrorist.

5. People in my family do not have politicians or public figures telling them they need to act more American.

6. My child can use the bathroom or locker room in which they feel most comfortable.

7. My child has more than a token adult in their school with whom they can identify, who has time and energy to mentor them.

8. My child can physically access the same spaces as others with little difficulty.

9. My child can go to college without wondering if others believe they got in because of affirmative action.

10. My family's holidays are celebrated or at least acknowledged by my child's school as much as those of other spiritual traditions.

11. My child can find comfortable and stylish clothing made for their body type.

12. My child can express political views without being accused of insufficient patriotism.

13. My child can access culturally competent health and mental health care.

14. I can reasonably assume my child will graduate high school and go on to receive some form of higher education.

15. My child can attend schools, drive down streets, and walk through parks that are not named for people who have oppressed their ancestors.

16. If my child gets in trouble, authorities would probably respect their rights and believe their side of the story.

17. My child can easily find toys and positive models in the media that reflect their identity.

18. People in my family can feel that the emergency personnel will actually provide assistance and not hurt them if they call 911.

19. I can access parenting books that are respectful of or relevant to my family's heritage and culture.

20. My child can get the appointments they need easily and with little financial hardship.

21. My child does not have people asking where they are "really" from.

22. My child can choose whether to spend time with other children like them or not.

23. My child does not have people asking what his or her "real" name or gender are.

24. My child can be assertive about their needs without fear of being labeled "angry," "crazy," or "dangerous."

25. My child can describe our family's personal (or professional) circumstances to others without fear of judgment or concern.

Just learning about privilege can inspire action, transforming compassion to a verb, as many teachers advise. One wealthy girl I see for therapy asked her parents if she could give up dessert and send the saved money to victims of the Haiti earthquake—she even convinced all the kids at her prep school to do the same, which resulted in thousands of dollars donated. McIntosh asks, "The question is, having described white privilege, what will I do to end it?" When we practice empathy and compassion, it sparks compassionate action in the real world.

reflection   What from the checklist resonated for you? What was hard to read? What privileges of your own could you add to the list?

Additional Suggestions and Practices

Lovingkindness meditation can be practiced in a myriad of formal ways, but here's a simple, informal exercise that is the basis of most compassion training. Try it as an entire family, when birthdays come around, or just before bed—really, try it any time you want, but make sure you practice these Kind Wishes in the order they appear.

PRACTICE   Kind Wishes

- First, bring to mind someone you deeply respect and look up to and who loves you in return. Think of something that would benefit this person and make them happy. Make a "kind wish" and send it their way.
- Next, send a wish to someone you love—a friend or family member.
- Now make a kind wish for a neutral person—someone you don't know very well at all (a person you often see in the grocery store, someone who delivers your mail, or a quiet neighbor, for example).
- Lastly, wish something nice for someone you dislike or feel frustrated with. (Or, as one teen I met put it, "Love your haters, man!")

The challenge is to begin with acts of compassion that come more naturally to us and then slowly expand the circle to include more difficult gestures of lovingkindness. I once heard Buddhist teacher Noah Levine describe it as starting with the little dumbbells in your life before moving on to the big dumbbells. Just as with physical training, we begin with actions that are easier.

Practices to foster connection and empathy can be found around the globe. Danish schools devote one hour per week for "Klassen time" to raise issues, resolve conflicts, and share treats. Christianity teaches the importance of asking for forgiveness and offering it to others. The Jewish holidays of Yom Kippur and Rosh Hashanah encourage reflection and reconciliation. Forgiveness is one of the six virtues in Hinduism. Even science has studied all of these to find ways to boost compassion and thus health and happiness.

Every two weeks, Thich Nhat Hanh's community engages in a "Beginning Anew" practice in which members share a ritual to resolve any conflict that may have arisen recently. This helps the community maintain a sense of health and wholeness, approaching themselves and each other with a fresh beginner's mind.[32] This practice can take place within a family or as a practice between parents or siblings. Whatever the constellation, participants agree to speak mindfully and listen without interrupting each other. It may help to have a third party present as a witness or facilitator to keep things on track. In fact, it's an excellent way to empower children in the facilitator role. Here are the three essential steps of Beginning Anew.

PRACTICE Beginning Anew

Flower Watering: In this part of the ritual, open with honest appreciation, naming specific actions and positive qualities of the other person, especially positive contributions within the family. In this way, you water the seeds of these positive qualities, turning minds and hearts toward the positive. This takes energy away from anger and misperception.

Sharing Regrets: In this next phase, express specific regrets, apologies to make, or amends to offer.

Expressing a Hurt: In the last phase, speak truthfully about how the other person's actions or words affected or hurt. When expressing the hurt, it is most effective to speak from a place of calm and compassion, perhaps by practicing some mindful breathing or walking beforehand.

Thich Nhat Hanh suggests that if we have a misunderstanding with someone, we wait until the person is finished speaking, even waiting a few days to clear things up. Best of all, he recommends a hugging meditation to close the ceremony.

We humans are meant to connect like this—our brains are wired for it. Mirror neurons activate when we watch another person, so that our bodies and brains literally feel what the other person is feeling and doing. This explains why we flinch when we see someone else in pain and why yawns, laughter, and strong emotions are contagious. The behaviors that our children witness in their families and communities will influence their values and development, right down to the level of their brain structure. How we interact and show love to our kids throughout their childhood—every criticism or gesture of kindness—creates a neurological template for their future relationships with friends, partners, and their own families, in turn.

When we don't cultivate compassion, it can wither in favor of our darker nature. A few months ago I spent a wonderful morning with Leo as he squealed and pointed with delight at some ants that had invaded the sidewalk in the wake of a dropped Popsicle. Yet only a week later he was ferociously stomping ants wherever he could find them. We can't always stop our kids from behaving unkindly, but we can encourage them to enact compassion and lovingkindness. Opportunities to do so arise all the time if we keep our eyes open. When we approach the world with mindfulness, we come to know it more deeply, and when we deeply know someone, it becomes hard not to love and care for them.

We don't have to be perfectly loving beings all the time. We don't have the financial, psychological, or genetic resources to treat everyone as we treat our child—let alone always treat our child how we'd like to. Trying to do so only leads to compassion fatigue, exhaustion, and burnout. When these occur, no matter the reason, it's time to go back to our own practice of self-compassion. If you have read this far, you are probably on the path to doing enough as a caring and compassionate parent, and that in itself may be enough. As always, do your best and strive for the middle path.

Compassion (even self-compassion) runs in families, so I encourage you to keep up the good work. In a study of social activists, altruistic kids were shown to carry the same values as their parents;[33] so what you do now really does make a difference. Remember that the lovingkindness your children received in the womb and early years of their life influences their brain structure and even how their genes are expressed, potentially affecting generations to come. Ashoka, the Buddhist emperor of India, followed a code that included respect for other faiths. His kingdom was known as the "kingdom of kindness." While few of us are modern-day emperors, perhaps we can strive to create a kingdom of kindness in ourselves, our families, and our communities.

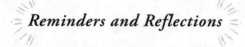

Reminders and Reflections

- If you engage in healthy self-compassion, you'll be much better at extending compassion inside and outside of your family.

- Not only is empathy an innate quality, but acts of compassion are also actually beneficial for our bodies and minds.

- What are some ways you can practice and model self-care and self-compassion in your life?

- What are ways you can help your children both tune into commonalities and appreciate differences with others?

- Find opportunities to try out the Self-Compassion, Beginning Anew, and Kind Wishes practices.

- Review the privileges you have that others don't, and find the right moment to discuss difficult issues such as privilege with your children.

- Give kids practical opportunities to exercise their innate kindness, like caring for plants or pets.

- Encourage your family to make eye contact and smile at people like clerks and waiters, wishing them a good day and *meaning it*.

CHAPTER 10

finding balance in a broken world and staying steady through the stress

(Raising Equanimity—Upekkha)

Early on in his teaching, the Buddha described life as 10,000 joys and 10,000 sorrows. As parents, each new day seems to bring *at least* another 10,000 home. The Buddha also mentioned something else most of us know to be true: life is stressful. Change and uncertainty are about the only constants we can depend on, and these can contribute to our suffering or our growth. Everything changes when we start a family, even down to our brain and hormones—in both women and men.[1] There is little more stressful, uncertain, and full of change than the ongoing process of parenting. And while change is hard for us parents to accept, growing up is not all fun and excitement for kids, either. Family legend has it that when I was two, I wailed inconsolably as deliverymen carried out our old refrigerator to deliver a brand new one. I'm still not so great with change and loss—the other day, I found myself holding back tears alongside my son when he lost his stuffed monkey.

So how do we deal with all this change? How do we abide the pains and joys of life—neither getting swept up in them nor turning our backs and ignoring them—and help our children learn to do the same? Traditionally, this quality of abiding is called *equanimity*, an attitude that is not to be mistaken for passivity or indifference, which are sometimes described as the "near enemies" of equanimity. When it comes to our family, equanimity is inextricably linked with compassion. We can have equanimity without compassion, like when we feel burned out and cynically dismiss our kids' concerns as mere manipulation. We can also have compassion without equanimity, responding to their immediate wants over their long-term needs because of our own intolerance of their discomfort. As I heard someone recently put it, compassion with equanimity means, "I want you to be happy, but I don't *need* you to be happy in order to be okay." Rather, equanimity is a radical acceptance of *not-knowing* and a means of not taking everything so personally. In meditation, we are often taught to recognize strong and difficult emotions as they arise without acting upon them, just like noticing the weather. We can do this with our loved ones as well, noting in our children, "Ah, anger is here. Sadness is here"—though, depending on the mood, perhaps not noting these thoughts aloud. In this way, we open ourselves to a deeper engagement with all of life, embodying balance and stability in the face of uncertainty and change. Most important, equanimity better enables us to develop a stable, secure base for attachment with our children, ensuring their optimal physical, psychological, and spiritual development.

The Eight Worldly Winds

Equanimity is said to keep us on the right track in the face of eight worldly winds—fame and disrepute (or praise and blame), gain and loss, success and failure, and joy and sorrow. We could all probably add a few more "winds" that we've experienced, but this list covers a great deal of what we face in life.

Buddhism teaches that the nature of suffering is dual and permeable, which is to say that we experience suffering together, and it's contagious. We are only as happy as our unhappiest child, as parents are fond of saying. And often, the stronger our bonds with our children, the more vividly we are blown about by their eight winds, experiencing their joys and sorrows in the complex dance of interpersonal neurobiology. One week our kids are invited to the "cool" party; the next, they are back with the "nerd herd." They win praise for their role in the winter musical but then are blamed for losing the playoff game by missing the fly ball. One spring they celebrate the success of acceptance to the college of their dreams, and the next fall they lose their scholarship when their grades slip. One bright summer day brings unbelievable joy at the beach but then inconsolable sorrow when their ice cream cone crashes onto the hot pavement. These delights, slings, and arrows come and go throughout their lives and our own. They also mirror each other. When our child is the difficult one at the playground, we watch as the other parents shrink away from us and playdate invitations fade. When our teen gets into trouble, we face the judgment of other parents who don't want their kids hanging out with our bad influence.

We too are certain to face these winds in the parenthood journey, if we haven't already. The day my son was due, my sister called to tell me she had been diagnosed with stage 2 breast cancer. One day our family has it all; the next day we lose a job, a house, or even a family member. One year we are the cool parent in our child's group of friends; the next we are infamously uptight and old-fashioned. Our own therapist praises our parenting, but our child's therapist gives us a long list of "suggestions." One year we celebrate our child's coming of age, the next we have to bury our own parents. The challenge in all of this is learning neither to overidentify with these changes nor to see them as permanent. The good news (and bad news) is that all the winds are temporary. Equanimity acts like the ballast of a ship. Although the ship is blown one way or the other by the winds of life, it neither sinks nor goes too far off-course.

reflection   Of these eight worldly winds, which has challenged you and your family the most? Which has been prominent for you in the past year? Which do you fear the most?

These eight worldly winds are also interdependent. For example, blame leads to shame, which calls for more self-compassion and self-forgiveness. Praise can encourage arrogance, which can be balanced by gratitude and appreciation for others. We can savor joy and pleasure and tolerate sorrow and pain all the better if we employ the wisdom of impermanence. We can balance success and failure by taking more personal responsibility, yet not taking it all personally. Let's look more closely at the eight winds and see how they play out in our lives.

Fame and Disrepute (Praise and Blame)

How well your family approaches and learns from these winds will determine your family's resilience. One of the best ways to deal with praise and blame is to be well-rounded, which is not the same as being hyperscheduled. You're more than a parent, just as your child is more than your son or daughter. Everyone in your family has multiple roles and activities that mean a lot to you—it's important to recognize that and to hold your identities lightly and enjoy them. To balance a ship, ballast must be spread evenly and widely.

If your child is overattached to their identity as the *smartest* kid or the *best* soccer player, they will struggle when the world inevitably suggests otherwise. This is often when they'll melt down, act out, or just give up on something that had been important to them. Even worse, they can become anxious and depressed, turn to drugs or cutting, or any number of other behaviors that land them in my office (or landed me in the offices of several therapists when I was a kid).

We can help them shift their identities in ways that will serve them in the long run. For example, we balance the identity of *smart kid* with the more sustainable identity of *hard worker*. Even better, we encourage kids in their various interests so they have a range of identities to fall back on. They might not get an A on the spelling test, but they're still a beloved grandchild, helpful friend, and decent skateboarder. Likewise, if they ace the test, they can feel great at something without overinflating their ego, because they're better able to put their successes in context with their more challenging endeavors like their one hard thing.

reflection   Are your family members' lives well-rounded enough to provide a cushion of confidence when things go wrong? In what ways are your lives dependent, independent, or interdependent on each other at this stage?

Gain and Loss

Just like praise and blame, gain and loss are inevitable parts of life from childhood onward. Although winning and losing streaks always end, we can accept the flow of victories and defeats. In addition—but admittedly trickier—we can learn to find silver linings when things don't go our way. One of my favorite teaching stories, *Sai and the Horse*, demonstrates these principles:

> Once, there was a farmer named Sai who lived with his family on their small farm. They were poor but had a horse to help with the labor in the fields, until one day in a storm, the horse ran away. The rest of the village came to console old Sai on his bad luck, but he merely replied, "Bad luck, good luck, who ever knows."
>
> The following week, the horse reappeared, this time with a mare in tow. The villagers shouted their congratulations. What great luck! In response, Sai merely smiled, "Good luck, bad luck, who ever knows."
>
> The next week, while training the new mare, Sai's son was thrown from the horse, falling to the ground and shattering his leg. Once more the villagers came to visit and share their condolences, and once more Sai simply shrugged and said, "Bad luck, good luck, who ever knows."
>
> Soon, a war broke out in the kingdom, and the king sent out a call for all able-bodied young men to join the army. All the young men of the village were killed, save for Sai's son, who had remained home with the broken leg. Once again, when congratulated on his good fortune, Sai simply said, "Good luck, bad luck, who ever knows."

Try sharing this story with your family in challenging times and good ones. You can also create new chapters to Sai's tale as you go, inviting your children to make up twists and turns of their own. Engaging the story on this level will highlight the value of acceptance; it also teaches us to look for the flower in the muck. Of course, broken legs and lost horses are one thing; it's much more difficult to remain calm and equanimous when we hear that 20 percent of our daughters are sexually assaulted by the time they finish college, and half of our sons will be in car accidents by the same age. But we can prepare ourselves and our children for the more difficult times to come by first working through the smaller challenges of skinned knees and broken hearts that will inevitably occur along the way.

We can practice equanimity much better when we understand how events are interdependent. We also develop equanimity when we look into the future with the same acceptance we have at examining the winding path that got us to where we are today. Equanimity arises when we renounce control—or, more accurately, when we renounce the illusion of control. Ideally, we learn along the way to strike a workable balance between letting our children live their own lives and make their own mistakes and keeping them happy and safe. Being a parent requires doing both.

reflection   Think of a time in your life when a success turned out to be more complicated or a loss turned out to be a surprise gain.

Success and Failure

It's natural to seek success in life and to want the same for our children. However, the dangers of success are arrogance and pride, which are often deficiencies in gratitude and the wisdom of interdependence. Fortunately, we can accompany any success we meet with mindful gratitude for others. A wise mentor once advised me, "Remember when you feel proud of an accomplishment to also feel grateful to those who helped you." That's why those Hollywood awards shows include "thank you" speeches and books include acknowledgments. We can model gratitude in the face of success with our children and point it out when we see the same happening in the world, helping them understand how their successes are built upon their relationships with others. By encountering success in this manner, we foster equanimity in all of us.

Setbacks are painful, but they too hold powerful lessons in equanimity. It's far too easy to become fixated on what failures seem to represent in the moment—not meeting an explicit goal or desire. It's much harder to see the bigger picture and take the long view. The truth is, the path to success is often circuitous, with plenty of failures along the way. Reflect on how this is true for you and share your journey with your children, or tell your kids stories about well-known people who had unexpected paths to success. People are often surprised to hear the route I took to get to where I am. I was an English major who took six years to finish my bachelors degree, after which I worked as a waiter, as an artist's assistant, at an Internet startup, and then as a special education teacher. I had absolutely no plans to become a child therapist; instead, I kind of fell into it after a series of what felt like major setbacks. I'd been rejected from graduate school at Harvard years ago, but I recently joined the faculty of Harvard Medical School. I could write an entire book on all the twists and turns in my life—as could you. Discuss your own setbacks, career changes, and odd meanderings with your kids—within reason, of course. Most important, reframe your so-called failures as opportunities. Doing so will help your children connect the dots between overcoming setbacks, staying true to one's values, hard work, and inevitable rewards.

None of us is immune to success and failure, even on a daily basis. Make it safe for your children to make mistakes. At around age five, kids begin to notice that adults have a negative emotional reaction to their mistakes, which unconsciously implies that they should be ashamed.[2] What we communicate to our children in the face of their blunders makes all the difference, just as how we model dealing with our own mistakes is important. Do we react to our defeats with shame and self-deprecation, or do we acknowledge them and get back to work? Some experts even recommend adults *deliberately* make mistakes and forgive themselves to model positive self-correction.

reflection What setbacks, disappointments, or unconventional aspects of your life path can you share with your children when they feel like giving up? How do you model mistakes to your family?

We all need to fail from time to time. Learning, adaptation, and resilience require some degree of defeat. It's not only okay to let your children fail; it's also wise to do so. Learning to bounce back from "failure" is one of the most useful gifts you can offer the adults they will eventually become. Only by making their way through smaller setbacks do our children learn how to deal with bigger setbacks.

When children do inevitably fail, it's critical that we don't place the blame on other people or circumstances out of their control—the muddy field, the biased referee, or the unfair teacher who has it in for them. Our kids will have to deal with these challenges in life, of course, but more important than recognizing these situations will be their sense of agency, autonomy, and responsibility. You can help them by compassionately talking through what *they* could do when such situations arise—practice in the mud, for example, or stay after class to ask the teacher for help. Even asking what they could have done to improve their experience of the past week will help them build a sense of autonomy to empower them to handle their next challenges with greater equanimity.

Joy and Sorrow, Pleasure and Pain

Humans are resilient. Consider the fact that our species has survived millennia of violence, disease, starvation, and emotional pain of all types. Even today, when something like 70 percent of people have experienced a traumatic event, only 20 percent of these survivors go on to develop PTSD.[3] And here's even more promising news: up to 90 percent of trauma survivors experience post-traumatic *growth*, which means they make meaning of the experience and transform themselves and others. Social psychologist James Pennebaker has shown that writing, visual arts, and other avenues of creative expression can help positively convert trauma, even boosting the psychological and physical immune systems.[4] He suggests using prompts like "I became stronger when I overcame _____," "I am the person I am because of _____," and "I am wiser now after _____" to help us transform the sorrows, traumas, and pains of life. We increase the benefit of doing so, of course, when we model this type of wise speech for our children.

As the Buddha famously pointed out, suffering is inevitable. None of us will escape sorrow and pain, not even people who devote their lives to the spiritual path. An interviewer once asked the Dalai Lama about his regrets in life. The holy man replied that after a student of his had once committed suicide, he had felt regret and responsibility for the man's death. When asked by the interviewer how to get rid of such a feeling, the Dalai Lama paused and then said, "I didn't. It's still there. I just don't allow it to drag me down and pull me back. I realized that being dragged down or held back by it would be to no one's benefit . . . not mine or anybody else's. So I go forward and do the best I can."[5] We're not trying to get rid of pain—ours or our children's. We can be saddened by pain, by our regrets and mistakes, and yet keep moving forward. This, too, is the wisdom of equanimity.

Comfort with Change and the Unknown

Equanimity is about appreciating the inevitability of change. It's about learning from everything we meet in life and growing through it all, which is pretty similar to the definition of resilience. Consider the number of changes you've had to make to become the parent you are today. What would your life be like if you refused to adapt to the rollercoaster of parenthood? When Leo was a few months old, he slept through the night, and my wife and I smugly assumed we had the best baby in the world. Well, that certainly changed. He went through a stretch of waking up every hour on the hour, but then that changed. And I'm just talking about his sleeping! The sleep thing was like a cosmic hazing ritual to prepare us for the ups and downs of the rest of parenthood—just when it becomes predictable, something changes and we have to adapt. Once Leo was sleeping, he was suddenly crawling everywhere and the house needed baby-proofing. Once the house was secured and he was no longer a danger, it was on to potty training, and on and on. It all reminds me of Sai's story.

The suffering emerges when we start assuming that how it is now is how it will be forever. When the baby is crying, we can get some relief from remembering that it will stop, eventually. Equanimity means letting go of our attachment to whatever arises, good or bad. Or as the saying goes, "Let go or be dragged." If we're too caught up in our dreams of our child going to Oxford someday, we'll suffer all the more (as will they) when they get their first B. It's not that we pour cold water on every exciting or good thing that comes along—I'm just suggesting that we all learn to take life's ups and downs in stride.

And what better practice for equanimity than parenthood? We're experts in dealing with change! Consider all the things that will change, from their sleep schedule, to their eating preferences, to their size and shape, their health, their mood. It will all change. So too will your relationship with your children and your partner. And guess what? The bad news is that the first year as parents is statistically likely to be our unhappiest, and becoming parents doesn't necessarily make us any happier.[6] But a year only lasts twelve months, and then things change again. Life doesn't always get better, but we can always get better at living it.

Reminders and Reflections

- Equanimity is a radical acceptance of *not-knowing* and a way of not taking everything so personally.

- Equanimity means renouncing the illusion of control.

- More trauma survivors experience post-traumatic growth than post-traumatic stress.

- Of the eight "worldly winds," which has challenged your family the most?

- What setbacks and surprises of your own life path can you share with your children when they face hardships?

- Encourage your children in multiple interests to help them have a range of strengths to fall back on.

- When you meet success in life, model gratitude with your children to illustrate equanimity and interdependence.

CONCLUSION

putting it all together

When I began to research and write this book, it seemed like a simple enough endeavor: ten spiritual principles and the research to back them up. But as I wrote, these virtues began to blur and blend, with the categories folding into each other. One of the challenges and delights of writing this book has been to see the connections throughout. Examining generosity closely, it begins to look a lot like kindness, both of which are really wise uses of our energy. Honesty is part of ethics, both of which are wise and compassionate. Renunciation is a wise use of energy, and how can it not be ethical to reduce our consumption, not to mention an act of compassion and generosity toward everyone else we share a planet with? Is waiting out the marshmallow patience, determination, or the wisest course of action? And doesn't each require—and result in—more equanimity? As you reflect on this wisdom and take it into the world, I encourage you to find ways in which aspects of one virtue emerge in the practice of another. In the end, these practices come together to build thriving, happy, resilient people, families, and communities, regardless of how we categorize them.

While each of these paramis is a universal spiritual principle, cutting across history and culture, they all are also scientifically validated. Spiritual traditions need not be incompatible with science. Ideally, they complement science, and science illustrates how these values help us evolve and grow into our best selves.

Remember also that this book is not about installing values in our children. Those values are there already—the seeds are planted in their hearts and etched into their DNA. Our kids need us to water those seeds, not force them. Looking at kids, it's easy to see that their fundamental nature is good, as one of the first markers of social development is the act of sharing. When I told a mentor how much I wanted my son to be good, he gently reminded me that it's far less about making him that way than keeping him that way—or as Rick Hanson says, "It takes time to become what we already are."

This book opened with an anecdote about how—upon becoming a parent—my own spiritual teacher encouraged me to forget my traditional meditation practice for a while and focus on living the paramis off of my comfortable meditation cushion. I've mostly tried to do that, but I still fit a moment in here or there for meditation practice. There's nothing like it to rewire our brains for resilience and respond with our best brains and bodies, rather than merely reacting to the organized chaos of parenthood. I recommend that you sneak in some sitting meditation. I'll close here with one of my favorite practices I've been cultivating these past few years since my son was born.

PRACTICE   Sleeping Child Meditation

Watch your child as they sleep, or use a picture of them if you're away from them. Take a few breaths and allow yourself to relax. Let your gaze soften as you take in the image of your child sleeping—that's your visual and emotional anchor for this practice. Notice their breathing and whatever movements or changes happen to their body as they sleep.

After a few moments of watching your child, turn your attention to yourself. Notice whatever feeling or reaction you're experiencing in the moment—love, pride, resentment, sleepiness, whatever. Just notice the experience, name it, and note when something different comes up. If your child stirs a little, maybe you become a little anxious that they're going to wake up. If they turn their body away from you, perhaps you feel the faintest chord of rejection. Whatever it is, let it arise and pass.

If your mind runs into the past or future, watch those thoughts as they come up, linger, and pass. Maybe you remember some aspect of their birth or look forward (perhaps with fear) to some future imagined event. Turn your mind toward the eight worldly winds you will experience together and that they will ultimately have to face on their own. These joys and sorrows, laughter and tears, will arise each and every day, whether you are physically with your child or not. Whatever comes to mind, let it arise and pass.

Now close your eyes again. Breathe. Send lovingkindness to your child. Use one of these phrases to promote equanimity, or perhaps just make kind wishes for them:

- You create your own life.
- Your joys and sorrows will be created through your relationship with the world, not through my relationship with the world.
- I will be here for you and with you throughout it all.
- Your freedom and happiness ultimately will depend on your actions, not my own.

Take a few more breaths, open your eyes, and take a moment before moving on to your next activity for the day.

Your child will experience so much in life, for a long time with you at their side but increasingly on their own. Ultimately, they must find and follow their own path. This whole parenting thing, as my friend put it, is one big process of letting go. As soon as they enter the world, we are instantly and forever connected in that moment of joy and pain. But from the time we first hold them in our arms, we begin the difficult business of letting go. And—who knows—maybe at the end of our lives, they're with us, holding our hand and helping us, in turn, let go of this world.

What can we hope to leave behind when that day comes? A child who can water more seeds of hope in themselves and their community, someone who can heal and soothe the suffering of the world, a person who changes hearts and minds, and someone who does the same for their children. As I watched my son come into this world, Thich Nhat Hanh's words rang in my mind: "Because you are alive, everything is possible."

As we think and act, so we create their world to come.

notes

Introduction

1. Elisha Goldstein, *Uncovering Happiness: Overcoming Depression with Mindfulness and Self-Compassion* (New York: Atria, 2015).

Chapter 1

1. Elizabeth W. Dunn, Lara B. Aknin, and Michael I. Norton, "Prosocial Spending and Happiness Using Money to Benefit Others Pays Off," *Current Directions in Psychological Science* 23, no. 1 (February 2014): 41–47.
2. Hidehiko Takahashi et al., "When Your Gain Is My Pain and Your Pain Is My Gain: Neural Correlates of Envy and Schadenfreude," *Science* 323, no. 5916 (February 2009): 937–39, doi: 10.1126/science.1165604.
3. Justin Fox, "Bush's Economic Mistakes: Telling Us to Go Shopping," *Time*, January 19, 2009, content.time.com/time/specials/packages/article/0,28804,1872229_1872230_1872236,00.html.
4. Nicholas A. Christakis and James H. Fowler, *Connected: The Surprising Power of Our Social Networks and How They Shape Our Lives* (New York: Little, Brown, 2009).
5. Jorge Moll et al., "Human Fronto-Mesolimbic Networks Guide Decisions about Charitable Donation," *Proceedings of the National Academy of Sciences* 103, no. 42 (2006): 15623–28, doi: 10.1073/pnas.0604475103.
6. Paul J. Zak, Angela A. Stanton, and Sheila Ahmadi, "Oxytocin Increases Generosity in Humans," *PLoS ONE* 2, no. 11 (2007), doi: 10.1371/journal.pone.0001128.

7. James Baraz and Shoshana Alexander, "The Helper's High," *Greater Good: The Science of a Meaningful Life*, February 1, 2010, greatergood.berkeley.edu/article/item/the_helpers_high/.

8. Elizabeth W. Dunn, Lara B. Aknin, and Michael I. Norton. "Spending money on others promotes happiness." *Science* 319, no. 5870 (2008): 1687–88.

9. Kathy Gilsinan, "The Buddhist and the Neuroscientist," *The Atlantic*, July 4, 2015, theatlantic.com/health/archive/2015/07/dalai-lama-neuroscience-compassion/397706/.

10. Sonja Lyubomirsky, *The How of Happiness: A Scientific Approach to Getting the Life You Want* (New York: Penguin Press, 2007).

11. Lara B. Aknin et al., "Prosocial Spending and Well-Being: Cross-Cultural Evidence for a Psychological Universal," *Journal of Personality and Social Psychology* 104, no. 4 (2013): 635–52.

12. Moll et al., "Human Fronto-Mesolimbic Networks."

13. Lyubomirsky, *The How of Happiness*.

14. Ron Lieber, "To Teach Children to Give, Tell Them How Much Your Family Has Been Given," *New York Times*, October 28, 2015, parenting.blogs.nytimes.com/2015/10/28/to-teach-children-to-give-tell-them-how-much-your-family-has-been-given/?smid=fb-nytimes&%3Bsmtyp=cur.

15. Paulina Pchelin and Ryan T. Howell, "The Hidden Cost of Value-Seeking: People Do Not Accurately Forecast the Economic Benefits of Experiential Purchases," *Journal of Positive Psychology* 9, no. 4 (2014): 322–34, doi: 10.1080/17439760.2014.898316.

16. Thich Nhat Hanh, *Living Buddha, Living Christ* (New York: Riverhead Books, 1995).

17. Epictetus, *A Manual for Living*, ed. Sharon Lebell (New York: HarperCollins, 1994).

18. Melinda Wenner Moyer, "How to Raise Generous Kids," *Slate*, December 18, 2015, slate.com/articles/life/the_kids/2015/12/how_to_raise_generous_kids_and_teach_empathy_and_charity_toward_the_poor.html.

19. Joan E. Grusec and Erica Redler, "Attribution, Reinforcement, and Altruism: A Developmental Analysis," *Developmental Psychology* 16, no. 5 (September 1980): 525–34, doi: 10.1037/0012-1649.16.5.525.

20. Stephanie B. Richman, C. Nathan DeWall, and Michelle N. Wolff, "Avoiding Affection, Avoiding Altruism: Why Is Avoidant Attachment Related to Less Helping?" *Personality and Individual Differences* 76 (April 2015): 193–97, doi: 10.1016/j.paid.2014.12.018.

Chapter 2

1. Suniya S. Luthar, Samuel H. Barkin, and Elizabeth J. Crossman, "'I Can, Therefore I Must': Fragility in the Upper-Middle Classes," *Development and Psychopathology* 25, no. 4pt2 (November 2013): 1529–49, doi: 10.1017/s0954579413000758.

2. Jennifer L. Hart and Michelle T. Tannock, "Playful Aggression in Early Childhood Settings," *Children Australia* 38, no. 3 (September 2013): 106–14, doi: 10.1017/cha.2013.14.

3. Anthony DeBenedet and Lawrence J. Cohen, *The Art of Roughhousing: Good Old-Fashioned Horseplay and Why Every Kid Needs It* (Philadelphia: Quirk Books, 2011).

4. Dan Ariely, *The (Honest) Truth about Dishonesty: How We Lie to Everyone—Especially Ourselves* (New York: Harper, 2012).

5. Christopher P. Krebs et al., "The Campus Sexual Assault (CSA) Study: Final Report" (2007), retrieved from the National Criminal Justice Reference Service, ncjrs.gov/pdffiles1/nij/grants/221153.pdf.

6. "The Healthy Sex Talk: Teaching Kids Consent, Ages 1–21," The Good Men Project, March 20, 2013, goodmenproject.com/families/the-healthy-sex-talk-teaching-kids-consent-ages-1-21/.

7. Albert Bandura, *Social Learning Theory* (Englewood Cliffs, NJ: Prentice-Hall, 1977).

8. Tom Shachtman, interviewed by Neil Conan, "Rumspringa: Amish Teens Venture into Modern Vices," *Talk of the Nation*, NPR, June 7, 2006, npr.org/templates/story/story .php?storyId=5455572.

9. Roy Baumeister and John Tierney, *Willpower: Rediscovering the Greatest Human Strength* (New York: Penguin Press, 2011).

10. Casey Baseel, "Divine Prevention: Japan Using Shinto Symbols to Combat Litter and Public Peeing," *Japan Today*, April 11, 2014, japantoday.com/category/lifestyle/view/ divine-prevention-japan-using-shinto-symbols-to-combat-litter-and-public-peeing.

11. Eric Schwitzgebel, "Do Ethicists Steal More Books?" *Philosophical Psychology* 22, no. 6 (2009): 711–25.

12. Uma R. Karmarkar and Bryan Bollinger, "BYOB: How Bringing Your Own Shopping Bags Leads to Treating Yourself and the Environment," *Journal of Marketing* 79, no. 4 (July 2015): 1–15, doi: 10.1509/jm.13.0228.

13. Sam K. Hui, Eric T. Bradlow, and Peter S. Fader, "Testing Behavioral Hypotheses Using an Integrated Model of Grocery Store Shopping Path and Purchase Behavior," *Journal of Consumer Research* 36, no. 3 (2009): 478–93, doi: 10.1086/599046.

14. Karmarkar and Bollinger, "BYOB."

15. Fengling Ma et al., "To Lie or Not to Lie? The Influence of Parenting and Theory-of-Mind Understanding on Three-Year-Old Children's Honesty," *Journal of Moral Education* 44, no. 2 (2015): 198–212.

16. John Bowlby, *Attachment*, 2nd ed. (New York: Perseus, 1982).

17. Sigmund Freud, *The Freud Reader* ed. Peter Gay (New York: Norton, 1995).

Chapter 3

1. Barry Schwartz, *The Paradox of Choice: Why More Is Less* (New York: Ecco, 2004).

2. Rick Weiss, "Study: U.S. Leads In Mental Illness, Lags in Treatment," *Washington Post*, June 7, 2005, washingtonpost.com/wp-dyn/content/article/2005/06/06/AR2005060601651.html.

3. Allison van Dusen, "How Depressed Is Your Country?" *Forbes*, February 16, 2007, forbes.com/2007/02/15/depression-world-rate-forbeslife-cx_avd_0216depressed.html.

4. Elizabeth Kolbert, "Spoiled Rotten: Why Do Kids Rule the Roost?" *New Yorker*, July 2, 2012, newyorker.com/magazine/2012/07/02/spoiled-rotten.

5. Jeanne E. Arnold, *Life at Home in the Twenty-First Century: 32 Families Open Their Doors* (Los Angeles: Cotsen Institute of Archaeology Press, 2012), 36.

6. Schwartz, *The Paradox of Choice.*

7. Kolbert, "Spoiled Rotten."

8. Howard Chudacoff, *Children at Play: An American History* (New York: New York University Press, 2007).

9. Kim John Payne, *Simplicity Parenting: Using the Extraordinary Power of Less to Raise Calmer, Happier, and More Secure Kids* (New York: Ballantine Books, 2009).

10. "Marketing to Children Overview," Campaign for a Commercial-Free Childhood, accessed December 22, 2016, commercialfreechildhood.org/resource/marketing-children-overview.

11. Marie Kondo, *The Life-Changing Magic of Tidying Up: The Japanese Art of Decluttering and Organizing* (Berkeley, CA: Ten Speed Press, 2014).

12. Madeleine Somerville, "Why Depriving Your Kids of Toys Is a Great Idea," *Guardian*, September 1, 2015, theguardian.com/global/2015/sep/01/depriving-your-kids-of-toys-great-idea.

13. Sarah Jewell, "The Nursery That Took All the Children's Toys Away," *Independent*, November 11, 1999, independent.co.uk/news/education/education-news/the-nursery-that-took-all-the-childrens-toys-away-1125048.html.

14. Andrew C. Hafenbrack, Zoe Kinias, and Sigal G. Barsade, "Debiasing the Mind Through Meditation: Mindfulness and

the Sunk-Cost Bias," *Psychological Science* 25, no. 2 (February 2014): 369–76, doi: 10.1177/0956797613503853.

15. Loyola University Health System, "Kids Who Specialize in One Sport May Have Higher Injury Risk," *ScienceDaily*, May 3, 2011, sciencedaily.com/releases/2011/05/110502121741.htm.

16. Kelly Wallace, "How much time do parents spend on their screens? As much as their teens," CNN, December 6, 2016, cnn.com/2016/12/06/health/parents-screen-use-attitudes-tweens-teens/.

17. Anna V. Sosa, "Association of the Type of Toy Used During Play with the Quantity and Quality of Parent-Infant Communication," *JAMA Pediatrics* 170, no. 2 (February 2016): 132–37, doi: 10.1001/jamapediatrics.2015.3753.

18. Robert Rosenthal and Lenore Jacobson, "Teachers' Expectancies: Determinants of Pupils' IQ Gains," *Psychological Reports* 19 (1966): 115–18, doi: 10.2466/pr0.1966.19.1.115.

19. M. A. Waltman et al., "The Effects of a Forgiveness Intervention on Patients with Coronary Artery Disease," *Psychology and Health* 24, no. 1 (January 2009): 11–27, doi: 10.1080/08870440903126371.

20. Megan Feldman Bettencourt, *Triumph of the Heart: Forgiveness in an Unforgiving World* (New York: Avery, 2015).

Chapter 4

1. Daniel J. Siegel and Tina Payne Bryson, *The Whole-Brain Child: 12 Revolutionary Strategies to Nurture Your Child's Developing Mind* (New York: Bantam Books, 2012).

2. Marsha Linehan, *Cognitive-Behavioral Treatment of Borderline Personality Disorder* (New York: Guildford, 1993).

3. Siegel and Bryson, *The Whole-Brain Child*.

4. Matthew D. Lieberman et al., "Putting Feelings into Words: Affect Labeling Disrupts Amygdala Activity in Response to Affective Stimuli," *Psychological Science* 18, no. 5 (May 2007): 421–28, doi: 10.1111/j.1467-9280.2007.01916.x.

5. Todd VanDerWerff, "Chart: How Inside Out's 5 Emotions Work Together to Make More Feelings," *Vox*, updated June 30, 2015, vox.com/2015/6/29/8860247/ inside-out-emotions-graphic.

6. Claudio Fernández-Aráoz, "Ignore Emotional Intelligence at Your Own Risk," *Harvard Business Review*, October 22, 2014, hbr.org/2014/10/ ignore-emotional-intelligence-at-you-own-risk.

7. Meagan E. Muller et al., "Gratitude and the Reduced Costs of Materialism in Adolescents," *PsycEXTRA Dataset*, doi: 10.1037/e711302011-001.

8. Tim Richards, "Kindness Can Exert Powerful Influence on World Around Us," *St. Louis Post-Dispatch*, September 6, 2004, 4.

9. Timothy D. Wilson et al., "Focalism: A Source of Durability Bias in Affective Forecasting," *Journal of Personality and Social Psychology* 78, no. 5 (May 2000): 821–36, doi: 10.1037//0022-3514.78.5.821.

10. Gretchen Reynolds, "To Better Cope with Stress, Listen to Your Body," *New York Times*, January 13, 2016, well.blogs.nytimes.com/2016/01/13/ to-better-cope-with-stress-listen-to-your-body/?_r=1.

Chapter 5

1. John Tierney, "Can a Playground Be Too Safe?" *New York Times*, July 18, 2011, nytimes.com/2011/07/19/ science/19tierney.html?_r=0.

2. Ibid.

3. Holly H. Schiffrin et al., "Helping or Hovering? The Effects of Helicopter Parenting on College Students' Well-Being," *Journal of Child and Family Studies* 23, no. 3 (April 2013): 548–57, doi: 10.1007/s10826-013-9716-3.

4. Laura M. Padilla-Walker and Larry J. Nelson, "Black Hawk Down? Establishing Helicopter Parenting as a Distinct

Construct from Other Forms of Parental Control During Emerging Adulthood," *Journal of Adolescence* 35, no. 5 (October 2012): 1177–90, doi: 10.1016/j .adolescence.2012.03.007.

5. Jane E. Barker et al., "Less-Structured Time in Children's Daily Lives Predicts Self-Directed Executive Functioning," *Frontiers in Psychology* 17, no. 5 (June 2014): 593, doi: 10.3389/fpsyg.2014.00593. eCollection 2014.

6. Terri LeMoyne and Tom Buchanan, "Does 'Hovering' Matter? Helicopter Parenting and Its Effect on Well-Being," *Sociological Spectrum* 31, no. 4 (2011): 399–418, doi: 10.1080/02732173.2011.574038.

7. Madeline Levine, *Teach Your Children Well: Parenting for Authentic Success* (New York: Harper, 2012).

8. Mihály Csíkszentmihályi, *Flow: The Psychology of Optimal Experience* (New York: Harper Perennial Modern Classics, 2009).

9. Payne, *Simplicity Parenting.*

10. Lindsay Hutton, "I Did It All by Myself! An Age-by-Age Guide to Teaching Your Child Life Skills," FamilyEducation .com, accessed February 6, 2017, life.familyeducation.com/ slideshow/independence/71434.html?page=1.

11. Andrew Moravcsik, "Why I Put My Wife's Career First," *Atlantic Monthly*, October 2015, theatlantic.com/magazine/ archive/2015/10/why-i-put-my-wifes-career-first/403240/.

12. Baumeister and Tierney, *Willpower.*

13. Ellen J. Langer, Arthur Blank, and Benzion Chanowitz, "The Mindlessness of Ostensibly Thoughtful Action: The Role of 'Placebic' Information in Interpersonal Interaction," *Journal of Personality and Social Psychology* 36, no. 6 (June 1978): 635–42, doi: 10.1037//0022-3514.36.6.635.

14. D. W. Winnicott, *The Child, the Family, and the Outside World* (Cambridge, Massachusetts: Perseus, 1964).

Chapter 6

1. Walter Mischel, *The Marshmallow Test: Mastering Self-Control* (New York: Little, Brown and Company, 2014).
2. Rick Hanson and Richard Mendius, *Buddha's Brain: The Practical Neuroscience of Happiness, Love, and Wisdom* (Oakland, CA: New Harbinger Publications, 2009).
3. Ibid.
4. Ibid.
5. J. David Creswell et al., "Neural Correlates of Dispositional Mindfulness During Affect Labeling," *Psychosomatic Medicine* 69, no. 6 (July-August 2007): 560–65, doi: 10.1097/PSY.0b013e3180f6171f.
6. Ellen J. Langer, *Mindfulness* (Boston: Addison-Wesley, 1989).
7. Paul Tough, "Can the Right Kinds of Play Teach Self-Control?" *New York Times*, September 25, 2009, nytimes.com/2009/09/27/magazine/27tools-t.html.
8. Pamela Druckerman, *Bringing Up Bébé* (New York: Penguin, 2012).
9. J. Roy Hopkins, "The Enduring Influence of Jean Piaget," *Observer*, December 2011, psychologicalscience.org/observer/jean-piaget#.WLco5Tw8KEc.

Chapter 7

1. Baumeister and Tierney, *Willpower*.
2. Ariely, *The (Honest) Truth about Dishonesty*.
3. Neil Garrett et al., "The Brain Adapts to Dishonesty," *Nature Neuroscience* 19, no. 12 (December 2016): 1727–32, doi: 10.1038/nn.4426.
4. Francesa Gino, Shahar Ayal, and Dan Ariely, "Contagion and Differentiation in Unethical Behavior: The Effect of One Bad Apple on the Barrel," *Psychological Science* 20, no. 3 (March 2009): 393–98, doi: 10.1111/j.1467-9280.2009.02306.x.
5. Ariely, *The (Honest) Truth About Dishonesty*.

6. "Academic Cheating Fact Sheet," Educational Testing Service/ Ad Council Campaign to Discourage Academic Cheating, last updated 1999, accessed December 22, 2016, glass-castle.com/clients/www-nocheating-org/adcouncil/research/cheatingfactsheet.html.

7. Lisa L. Shu et al., "Signing at the Beginning Makes Ethics Salient and Decreases Dishonest Self-Reports in Comparison to Signing at the End," *Proceedings of the National Academy of Sciences* 109, no. 38 (September 2012): 15197–200, doi: 10.1073/pnas.1209746109.

8. Xiao Pan Ding et al., "Theory-of-Mind Training Causes Honest Young Children to Lie," *Psychological Science* 26, no. 11 (November 2015): 1812–21, doi: 10.1177/0956797615604628.

9. Victoria Talwar and Kang Lee, "Development of Lying to Conceal a Transgression: Children's Control of Expressive Behaviour During Verbal Deception," *International Journal of Behavioral Development* 26, no. 5 (September 2002): 436–44 doi: 10.1080/01650250143000373.

10. Kang Lee et al., "Can Classic Moral Stories Promote Honesty in Children?" *Psychological Science* 25, no. 8 (August 2014): 1630–36 doi: 10.1177/0956797614536401.

11. Ayelet Gneezy and Daniel Ariely, "Don't Get Mad Get Even: On Consumers' Revenge" (unpublished manuscript, Duke University, 2010).

12. Po Bronson and Ashley Merryman, *NurtureShock: New Thinking about Children* (New York: Twelve, 2009), 83–84.

13. Victoria Talwar and Angela Crossman, "From Little White Lies to Filthy Liars: The Evolution of Honesty and Deception in Young Children," *Advances in Child Development and Behaviour* 40, no. 140 (2011): 139–79.

14. Jane Nelsen, "Bullying on the Bus," *Positive Discipline* (blog), accessed December 22, 2016, positivediscipline.com/articles/bullying-bus.

15. Carolyn Zahn-Waxler, Marian Radke-Yarrow, and Robert A. King, "Child Rearing and Children's Prosocial Initiations

toward Victims of Distress," *Child Development* 50, no. 2 (June 1979): 319–30, doi: 10.2307/1129406.

16. Martin L. Hoffman, "Altruistic Behavior and the Parent-Child Relationship," *Journal of Personality and Social Psychology* 31, no. 5 (May 1975): 937–43, doi: 10.1037/h0076825.

Chapter 8

1. Carol S. Dweck, *Mindset: The New Psychology of Success* (New York: Random House, 2006).
2. Angela Duckworth, *Grit: The Power of Passion and Perseverance* (New York: Scribner, 2016).
3. Daniel Pink, *Drive: The Surprising Truth About What Motivates Us* (New York: Riverhead Books, 2009).
4. Alfie Kohn, *Punished by Rewards: The Trouble with Gold Stars, Incentive Plans, A's, Praise, and Other Bribes* (New York: Houghton Mifflin, 1993).
5. Editorial, "Should Allowances Be Tied to Chores?" *Wall Street Journal*, May 14, 2012, wsj.com/articles/SB10001424052702 3044327045773497112481263398.
6. Langer, *Mindfulness*.
7. Eddie Brummelman et al., "Origins of Narcissism in Children," *Proceedings of the National Academy of Sciences* 112, no. 12 (2015): 3659–62.
8. Bronson and Merryman, *NurtureShock*.
9. Claudia M. Mueller and Carol S. Dweck, "Praise for Intelligence Can Undermine Children's Motivation and Performance," *Journal of Personality and Social Psychology* 75, no. 1 (July 1998): 33–52.
10. Lisa S. Blackwell, Kali H. Trzesniewski, and Carol Sorich Dweck, "Implicit Theories of Intelligence Predict Achievement across an Adolescent Transition: A Longitudinal Study and an Intervention," *Child Development* 78, no. 1 (2007): 246–63, doi: 10.1111/j.1467-8624.2007.00995.x.

11. Po Bronson, "How Not to Talk to Your Kids," *New York Magazine*, August 3, 2007nymag.com/news/features/27840/.

12. Ibid.

13. Baumeister and Tierney, *Willpower*.

14. Ami Albernaz, "Sparing the Chores Spoils Children and Their Future Selves, Study Says," *Boston Globe*, December 8, 2015, bostonglobe.com/lifestyle/2015/12/08/research-indicates-sparing-chores-spoils-children-and-their-future-selves/ZLvMznpC5btmHtNRXXhNFJ/story.html.

15. University of Minnesota, "Involving Children in Household Efforts: Is It Worth It?" September 2002, accessed February 6, 2017, ghk.h-cdn.co/assets/cm/15/12/55071e0298a05_-_Involving-children-in-household-tasks-U-of-M.pdf.

16. George E. Vaillant, "Natural History of Male Psychological Health III: Empirical Dimensions of Mental Health," *Archives of General Psychiatry* 32, no. 4 (1975): 420–26, doi: 10.1001/archpsyc.1975.01760220032003.

17. Baumeister and Tierney, *Willpower*.

18. KJ Dell'Antonia, "Raising a Child with Grit Can Mean Letting Her Quit," *New York Times*, April 29, 2016, well.blogs.nytimes.com/2016/04/29/when-raising-a-child-with-grit-means-letting-her-quit/.

19. Margo Gardner, Jodie Roth, and Jeanne Brooks-Gunn, "Adolescents' Participation in Organized Activities and Developmental Success 2 and 8 Years after High School: Do Sponsorship, Duration, and Intensity Matter?" *Developmental Psychology* 44, vol. 3 (May 2008): 814–30, doi: 10.1037/0012-1649.44.3.814.

20. Baumeister and Tierney, *Willpower*.

21. Ethan Kross et al., "Self-Talk as a Regulatory Mechanism: How You Do It Matters," *Journal of Personality and Social Psychology* 106, no. 2 (February 2014): 304–24, doi: 10.1037/a0035173.

Chapter 9

1. Joel Lovell, "George Saunders's Advice to Graduates," The 6th Floor (blog), *New York Times*, July 31, 2013, 6thfloor.blogs.nytimes.com/2013/07/31/george-saunderss-advice-to-graduates/?_r=0.

2. Shelley Taylor et al., "Biobehavioral Responses to Stress in Females: Tend-and-Befriend, not Fight-or-Flight," *Psychological Review*, 107, no. 3 (July 2000): 411–29.

3. Kelly April Tyrrell, "'Kindness Curriculum' Boosts School Success in Preschoolers," *University of Wisconsin–Madison News*, January 23, 2015, news.wisc.edu/kindness-curriculum-boosts-school-success-in-preschoolers/.

4. Kristin D. Neff and Christopher K. Germer, "A Pilot Study and Randomized Controlled Trial of the Mindful Self-Compassion Program," *Journal of Clinical Psychology*, 69, no. 1 (January 2013): 28–44, doi: 10.1002/jclp.21923.

5. Susan Bögels, "Mindful Parenting: A Mindfulness Course for Parents in Mental Health Treatment," in *Teaching Mindfulness Skills to Kids and Teens*, ed. Christopher Willard and Amy Saltzman (New York: The Guilford Press, 2015).

6. Paul Bloom, "The Moral Life of Babies," *New York Times*, May 5, 2010, nytimes.com/2010/05/09/magazine/09babies-t.html?_r=0.

7. Damon E. Jones, Mark Greenberg, and Max Crowley, "Early Social-Emotional Functioning and Public Health: The Relationship between Kindergarten Social Competence and Future Wellness," *American Journal of Public Health* 105, no. 11 (November 2015): 2283–90, doi: 10.2105/ajph.2015.302630.

8. Kate Murphy, "What Selfie Sticks Really Tell Us about Ourselves," *New York Times*, August 8, 2015, nytimes.com/2015/08/09/sunday-review/what-selfie-sticks-really-tell-us-about-ourselves.html.

9. Barbara L. Fredrickson et al., "Open Hearts Build Lives: Positive Emotions, Induced through Loving-Kindness

Meditation, Build Consequential Personal Resources," *Journal of Personality and Social Psychology* 95, no. 5 (November 2008): 1045–62, doi: 10.1037/a0013262.

10. James W. Carson et al., "Loving-Kindness Meditation for Chronic Low Back Pain: Results from a Pilot Trial," *Journal of Holistic Nursing* 23, no. 3 (September 2005): 287–304, doi: 10.1177/0898010105277651.

11. Makenzie E. Tonelli and Amy B. Wachholtz, "Meditation-Based Treatment Yielding Immediate Relief for Meditation-Naïve Migraineurs," *Pain Management Nursing* 15, no. 1 (March 2014): 36–40, doi: 10.1016/j .pmn.2012.04.002.

12. David J. Kearney et al., "Loving-Kindness Meditation for Posttraumatic Stress Disorder: A Pilot Study," *Journal of Traumatic Stress* 26, no. 4 (August 2013): 426–34, doi: 10.1002/jts.21832.

13. Paul Condon et al., "Meditation Increases Compassionate Responses to Suffering," *Psychological Science* 24, no. 10 (October 2013): 2125–27, doi: 10.1177/0956797613485603.

14. Richard Alleyne, "Holding Hands Reduces Pain," *The Telegraph*, November 15, 2009, telegraph.co.uk/news/science/ science-news/6575716/Holding-hands-reduces-pain.html.

15. Barbara Bradley Hagerty, "Midlife Friendship Key to a Longer, Healthier Life," *Morning Edition*, NPR, March 26, 2016, npr.org/2016/03/16/470635733/ midlife-friendship-key-to-a-longer-healthier-life.

16. Helen Y. Weng et al., "Compassion Training Alters Altruism and Neural Responses to Suffering," *Psychological Science* 24, no. 7 (July 2013): 1171–80, doi: 10.1177/0956797612469537.

17. Condon et al., "Meditation Increases Compassionate Responses to Suffering."

18. Gilsinan, "The Buddhist and the Neuroscientist."

19. Sara H. Konrath, Edward H. O'Brien, and Courtney Hsing, "Changes in Dispositional Empathy in American College

Students Over Time: A Meta-Analysis," *Personality and Social Psychology Review* 15, no. 2 (May 2011): 180–98, doi: 10.1177/1088868310377395.

20. Making Caring Common Project, *The Children We Mean to Raise* (Cambridge, MA: Harvard Graduate School of Education), sites .gse.harvard.edu/sites/default/files/making-caring-common/files/ mcc_the_children_we_mean_to_raise_4.pdf.

21. Condon et al., "Meditation Increases Compassionate Responses to Suffering."

22. Philip Zimbardo, *The Lucifer Effect: Understanding How Good People Turn Evil* (London: Rider Books, 2007).

23. Sylvia Boorstein, *Pay Attention for Goodness' Sake: Practicing the Perfections of the Heart—The Buddhist Path of Kindness* (New York: Ballantine, 2002).

24. John M. Darley and C. Daniel Batson, "'From Jerusalem to Jericho': A Study of Situational and Dispositional Variables in Helping Behavior," *Journal of Personality and Social Psychology* 27, no. 1 (July 1973): 100–8.

25. James H. Fowler and Nicholas A. Christakis, "Cooperative behavior cascades in human social networks," *Proceedings of the National Academy of Sciences* 107, no. 12 (January 2010): 5334–38, doi: 10.1073/pnas.0913149107.

26. Mirabai Bush, "Just Like Me Meditation," available for download via Ram Dass' December Retreat Resource Page, posted December 15, 2014, ramdass.org/ december-retreat-resource-page/.

27. Thich Nhat Hanh, *How to Love* (Berkeley, CA: Parallax, 2014).

28. Celia A. Brownell et al., "Socialization of Early Prosocial Behavior: Parents' Talk about Emotions Is Associated with Sharing and Helping in Toddlers," *Infancy* 18, no. 1 (January-February 2013): 91–119, doi: 10.1111/j.1532-7078.2012.00125.x.

29. Pamela W. Garner, "Child and Family Correlates of Toddlers' Emotional and Behavioral Responses to a Mishap," *Infant*

Mental Health Journal 24, no. 6 (November/December 2003): 580–596, doi: 10.1002/imhj.10076.

30. Adam Lueke and Bryan Gibson, "Mindfulness Meditation Reduces Implicit Age and Race Bias: The Role of Reduced Automaticity of Responding," *Social Psychological and Personality Science* 6, no. 3 (2015), doi: 1948550614559651.

31. "White Privilege Checklist," Creative Response to Conflict, June 2012, crc-global.org/wp-content/uploads/2012/06/white-privilege.pdf.

32. Thich Nhat Hanh, *Teachings on Love* (Berkeley, CA: Parallax, 1997).

33. David Rosenhan, "Some Origins of Concern for Others," *ETS Research Bulletin Series* 1968, no. 1 (June 1968): i–43, doi: 10.1002/j.2333-8504.1968.tb00557.x.

Chapter 10

1. Benedetta Leuner, Erica R. Glasper, and Elizabeth Gould, "Parenting and Plasticity," *Trends in Neurosciences* 33, no. 10 (October 2010): 465–73, doi: 10.1016/j.tins.2010.07.003.

2. Dweck, *Mindset: The New Psychology of Success.*

3. "Post-Traumatic Stress Disorder Fact Sheet," Sidran Institute, accessed February 6, 2017, sidran.org/resources/for-survivors-and-loved-ones/post-traumatic-stress-disorder-fact-sheet/.

4. James W. Pennebaker, "Writing about Emotional Experiences as a Therapeutic Process," *Psychological Science* 8, no. 3 (May 1997): 162–166, doi: 10.1111/j.1467-9280.1997.tb00403.x.

5. Pema Chodron, *Getting Unstuck* (Boulder, CO: Sounds True, 2005), audio recording, 3 CDs.

6. Mikko Myrskylä and Rachel Margolis, "Happiness: Before and After the Kids," *Demography* 51, no. 5 (2014): 1843–66, doi: 10.1007/s13524-014-0321-x.

acknowledgments

This book has one author, but it took many, many people to write. Very few of the ideas presented here are original—mostly they're evolutions of existing research or teachings or that wisdom somehow placed in a new light. This book looks at ancient wisdom and compares it to other people's research, much of which was directed my way by some incredible writers and teachers, all of whom deserve thanks.

First, the underlying idea for this book was inspired by Maddy Kline, my teacher at Cambridge Insight Meditation Center. I also want to begin by thanking my wife and family for dealing with the countless hours of writing and researching, as well as all the time away from them. My parents and sister, for teaching me how to be a parent. Next, everyone at Sounds True—from Tami Simon (who has inspired me for decades) to Jennifer Brown (who offered the contract on the manuscript) to Robert Lee (who edited it) to Tara Joffe (my copyeditor)—as well as all the production and marketing staff along the way. All of them helped make this beautiful object in your hands. I also can't thank Carol Mann, my agent, enough for getting the deal done.

Several friends and colleagues took glances at chapters and offered feedback. My wife, Olivia Weisser, and friends Mark Bertin, Ebru Engin, and Mitch Abblett, in particular, gave the book thorough readings and feedback. Other friends helped with certain sections— Jameson Beekman, Ariel Brown, Tim Desmond, Vanessa Gobes, Betsy Hanger, Margaret Lewis, Anne Moore, Sarah Reid, and Hannah Sharpless. Fabio Marcovski helped a ton with citations and research.

There are people whose words and spirit appear in these pages—clients and friends in composite form. Thanks to Ariel Brown, Harris Danow, Julia Daunis, Scott Dvorin, Chris Germer, Bob and Fiona Jensen, Francis Kolarik, Susan Pollak, Samantha Smith, Zack Whedon, Edward Yeats, and more. My colleagues at

Cambridge Hospital, The Center for Mindfulness and Compassion, Harvard Medical School, the Institute for Meditation and Psychotherapy, and friends in the Mindfulness in Education Network have all inspired me. The Insight Meditation Society of Pioneer Valley parenting sangha has also been a source of inspiration.

Then there are the authors and writers whose work pointed me to the good stuff. Thich Nhat Hanh was my first teacher on these matters and remains a powerful inspiration. I hope I honor his spirit as it echoes through the book. Pema Chödrön, Jack Kornfield, Tara Brach, Sylvia Boorstein, Sharon Salzberg, and others are inspirations on the spiritual front.

Then there are the writers who did the work of finding the primary research, saving me time as I savored their books and raided their bibliographies. This book was most inspired by Rick Hanson's work. Kim John Payne and Lisa Ross's *Simplicity Parenting* shared ideas and research about, well, simplification, as did Marie Kondo's *The Life-Changing Magic of Tidying Up*. Po Bronson and Ashley Merryman's *NurtureShock* introduced me to Carol Dweck's research and her book *Mindset*, as well as fascinating insights into why kids lie. Dan Siegel and Tina Payne Bryson eloquently broke down the science of the developing brain with their "upstairs/downstairs" model of the brain in *The Whole-Brain Child*. Julie Lythcott-Haimes's *How to Raise an Adult* is not just a brilliant title but also a brilliant resource on resilience. Walter Mischel's research and related work was so beautifully captured by his book *The Marshmallow Test*, which inspired much of the chapter on patience. Mihály Csíkszentmihályi's work on flow and creativity deeply informed a number of chapters, and Angela Duckworth's *Grit* compiled so much research on determination, as did Roy Baumeister and John Tierney's *Willpower*, Kelly McGonigal's writing, and Daniel Pink's *Drive*. Dan Ariely's amazing *The (Honest) Truth about Dishonesty* is also rich in research on truth and lies. Lisa Miller's research descriptions in *The Spiritual Child* were another treasure trove, and Elisha Goldstein's *Uncovering Happiness* was a fantastic resource. Melinda Moyer, the wonderful parenting writer at Slate.com, also culled some useful research on topics like apologies, aggression, and more.

about the author

Christopher Willard, PsyD, is a psychologist and consultant based in Boston who works with individuals, schools, hospitals, and other organizations. He is the author of multiple books on psychology, child development, and contemplative practice. He currently serves as the president of the Mindfulness in Education Network and sits on the board of directors at the Institute for Meditation and Psychotherapy. He leads courses and workshops around the world and online, in addition to teaching at Harvard Medical School. His TEDx talks appear on his website—drchristopherwillard.com—where you can also learn more about his work and events and get in touch. You can also stay up to date on Facebook and Twitter @drchriswillard.

about sounds true

Sounds True is a multimedia publisher whose mission is to inspire and support personal transformation and spiritual awakening. Founded in 1985 and located in Boulder, Colorado, we work with many of the leading spiritual teachers, thinkers, healers, and visionary artists of our time. We strive with every title to preserve the essential "living wisdom" of the author or artist. It is our goal to create products that not only provide information to a reader or listener, but that also embody the quality of a wisdom transmission.

For those seeking genuine transformation, Sounds True is your trusted partner. At SoundsTrue.com you will find a wealth of free resources to support your journey, including exclusive weekly audio interviews, free downloads, interactive learning tools, and other special savings on all our titles.

To learn more, please visit SoundsTrue.com/freegifts or call us toll-free at 800.333.9185.